My Reminiscences of Guru Dev

I0541560

Swami Brahmananda Saraswati

A Perfect Yogi and Divine Saint (1870-1953)

JUGAL KISHOR SHRIVASTAVA

My Reminiscences of Guru Dev
First Edition
Published by the Guru Dev Legacy Trust,
New York, New York, USA
Copyright © 2025 by Sanjay Shrivastava
Raipur Chhattisgarh India
email: umeshryp04@gmail.com

This book may not be reproduced in whole or in part by any means without the expressed written permission of Sanjay Shrivastava.

Note: Persons interested in learning more about the Guru Dev Legacy Trust, or who would like to support the Trust's translation of yet unpublished discourses of Guru Dev, are invited to visit the Trust's website at www.gurudevlegacytrust.com.

ISBN: 979-8-9915588-0-8 (Paperback)
ISBN: 979-8-9915588-2-2 (Hardcover)
ISBN: 979-8-9915588-1-5 (eBook)

To the Lotus Feet of Guru Dev

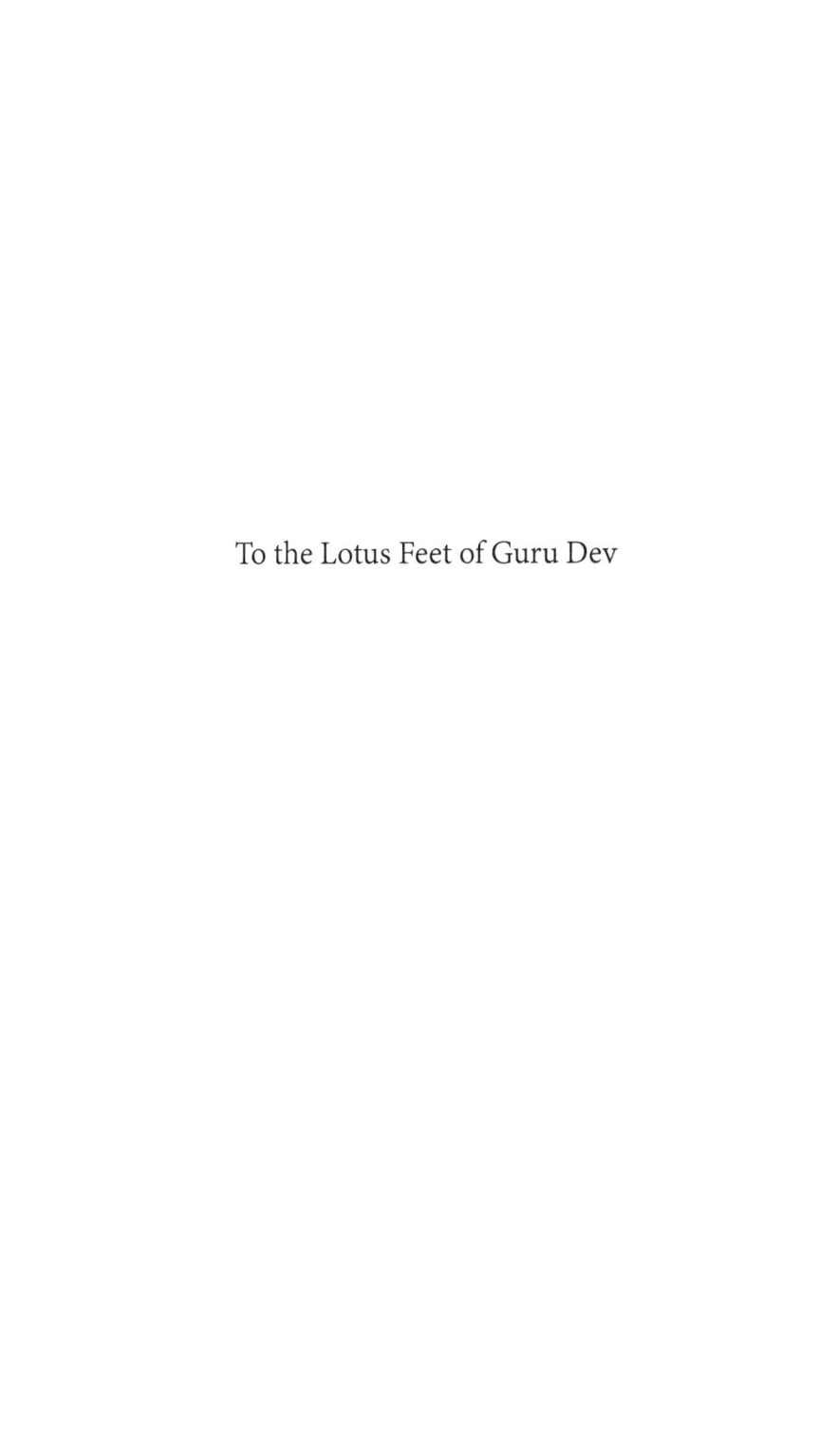

Contents

Publisher's Preface

THE Guru Dev Legacy Trust is pleased to publish the reminiscences of a disciple of Swami Brahmananda Saraswati, a highly revered Indian saint who served as Śaṅkarācārya of Jyotir Maṭh, the highest position of spiritual leadership in north India.

Swami Brahmananda ushered in a major spiritual revival throughout India, restoring spiritual truth in all its purity and simplicity. He was seen as the harmoniser and unifier of all schools of belief and was heralded by the president of India as "Vedanta Incarnate," the very embodiment of Supreme Truth. After his passing, his revival was continued by his followers, including Maharishi Mahesh Yogi, who spread the practice of Transcendental Meditation around the world for over sixty years.

The Guru Dev Legacy Trust was formed in 2014 to locate, preserve and archive materials pertaining to Swami Brahmananda's life and teaching. While transcripts of many of Swami Brahmananda's spoken discourses were preserved, there appeared to be few written or recorded recollections of him by his followers, other than those of Maharishi Mahesh Yogi. The Trust was therefore pleased to learn several years ago that another of Swami Brahmananda's disciples, Jugal Kishor Shrivastava (1902-1970), wrote of his experiences and interactions with this great sage. His reminiscences, handwritten in Hindi, were carefully preserved by his son, Umesh Shrivastava, and now by his grandson, Sanjay Shrivastava.

Jugal's reminiscences provide us with delightful insights into the kind and compassionate way in which Swami Brahmananda guided his followers, including householder disciples like Jugal. In reading Jugal's reminiscences, we are given glimpses into the time-honoured Vedic tradition of master and disciple.

The Shrivastava family long wished to have Jugal's reminiscences translated and published in English. The family asked the Trust to undertake this task and the Trust happily agreed. Umesh and Sanjay subsequently joined the Trust's board of directors and invited the Trust's three western board members to visit their family home in Raipur, India in April of 2019. Many happy hours were spent together, with visits to local temples and the birth site of Maharishi Mahesh Yogi in a rural village several hours drive away. Umesh wrote of the close friendship that developed with the western board members, stating "I strongly believe that there exists an eternal bond between us that has resulted in this memorable confluence of the West and the East."

Umesh's devotion to Swami Brahmananda was deep. It guided his thoughts, words and deeds in a natural and spontaneous way. In the Indian spiritual tradition, the guru is likened to the electrical power station to which the disciple can connect at any time. Umesh clearly had made that connection. Basking in his joyful presence, we felt our own connection with Swami Brahmananda deeply enlivened.

Umesh Shrivastava

Umesh passed away on December 4, 2021, before this book was completed. Fortunately, he was able to review an early proof and was joyful in the knowledge that his father's reminiscences would become available to people everywhere.

We have included an Appendix of supplemental materials that provide a fuller context for the reminiscences. These include a tribute to Shrivastava family, various historical letters to the Shrivastava family, a short biography of Swami Brahmananda, and a selection of Swami Brahmananda's discourses.

The teachings of Swami Brahmananda are simple, yet deeply profound. They are universal in nature and can benefit people of all nationalities, religious traditions and walks of life. The Shrivastava family and the Trust hope that this book will inspire its readers and provide them with valuable guidance on their journey toward spiritual realisation.

The western members of the Guru Dev Legacy Trust with the Shrivastava family in Raipur, India in April of 2019. The present board members of the Trust are, from left to right in the back row, Daniel Friedman (USA), Robert Sanders (USA), Lothar Heggmair (Germany) and Sanjay Shrivastava (India).

Translator's Note

THE original text of *Reminiscences* was written in Hindi using the Devanāgarī script and included some Sanskrit terms. The Trust took great care to produce an accurate translation that captures, to the extent possible, the meaning of the original Hindi text.

The translator has used the international standard of IAST (International Alphabet of Sanskrit Transliteration) for the transliteration of the Devanāgarī script to English. The only exceptions are some Sanskrit or Hindi words that are commonly known. For these we have used the simplified English notation in common use.

IAST is favored among by scholars and linguists because it provides a precise Romanisation of Indic scripts found in Sanskrit and related Indic languages, including Hindi. IAST uses diacritics to disambiguate phonetically similar but not identical Sanskrit glyphs. As such, it allows the reader to read the Indic text exactly as if it were in the original Indic script, allowing the reader to discover the beauty of the sound of the original words and phrases. This is particularly important, in the Indian tradition, the sound of a word or phrase is integrated with its meaning (nāma and rūpa are equivalent in a spiritual sense). IAST also facilitates further research because the terms appear as they do in Sanskrit dictionaries and in scholarly works.

To aid the reader, we include below several basic rules of pronunciation in IAST methodology.

- Hindi vowels have both short forms and lengthened forms, the latter are transliterated by a line over the vowel (ā ī ū).

- Consonants have both aspirated forms (kh, gh, ch, jh) and unaspirated forms (k, g, c, j).

- There is also a set of retroflexes, which have no precise English equivalents, and these are transliterated with a dot beneath (ṭ ṭh ḍ ḍh ṇ). They involve curling the tongue farther back onto the roof of the mouth than for the English dentals.

- ś as in "shove" and ṣ as in "crashed," but with the tongue curled farther back.

CHAPTER 1

The Torch of Knowledge

INVOCATION TO LORD RĀMA

He who is the abode of all happiness and removes all unhappiness, He who used to dwell playfully in King Dasarat's courtyard, please show mercy on me.

—Rāmcaritmānas (1-11-2)[1]

THAT day was the golden morning of my life. It was the autumn of 1942. In the outer world, the dependent, but freedom-fighting India rose up to break the bondages of slavery. The very heart of the foreign government began to tremble and the foundation of the dreadful prison was shaken. The dense darkness of the night of the first moon lifted.

In this exciting atmosphere, filled with the expectation of freedom and independence, there

1 Rāmcaritmānas – an epic poem about Śrī Rām in the Avadhī language, composed by the Indian bhakti poet Goswami Tulsidas (1532-1623).

arose in India an alert and vigilant national consciousness that propelled events. With the dawn of the sun rising in the East, a deep sense of auspiciousness started to rise.

I was not left untouched by the exhilarating effect of this auspicious moment. The slothful anguish of my confused life spread its wings, darted from its nest, flew into a remote corner of the vast firmament and disappeared forever. The drowsy life stretched and opened its eyes and, as the eyelids lifted, a procession appeared opposite, moving from near the great Mahāvīr toward Baldev Bāg in Jabalpur.

The sound of conches and bells filled the air, along with cries of "Glory to Jagadguru Bhagvān Śaṅkarācārya Jyotiṣpīṭhādhīśvar Bhagvān!," "Hail to the Indestructible World Teacher," "Hail to the Feet of the Ācārya!"

I stood paralyzed beside the street, watching and hearing everything, when Mahārājśrī came into sight. How can I describe the unprecedented effect this had on me? Unbounded bliss began to arise in my innermost being. My long unsatisfied thirst was quenched. It was as though the guest of the eyes—for whom I had revolved for ages carrying my hopes and longings to offer Him a welcoming shawl—had at last arrived. The overflowing compassion of the heart and the priceless pearl of devotion—woven together with the colourful flowers of rapture and faith—formed a welcome garland that I mentally offered, with myself, at the feet of Śrī Ācāryacaraṇ.[2]

In this stony, senseless heart, how did these charming, soft, sweet-smelling flowers bloom? In this desert, on the easterly wind of boundless faith, from where and how did such surrender overflow with such a deeply charming sound? Hearing it, the crow-like mind was transformed into a peacock and began to dance. Who played this sweet flute in the wild region? Aah, who will be able to solve that mystery? Whatever the mystery may be, the effect of the darśan[3] was unmistakable.

Upon inquiring, I learned that I was beholding the Jagadguru of Jyotir Maṭh, who had been installed the prior year on the holy throne of Śaṅkarācārya of the Badrikāśram. This divine seat, which had been vacant for 165 years, was now beautified by Mahārājśrī.

On the west side of the city Jabalpur there is a beautiful garden called Baldev Bāg with a building on one side. In this building was the camp of Mahārājśrī. Among the devotees gathered there were all kinds of people: ascetics, scholars, renunciates and householders. All stayed in the

2 Teacher's or guru's feet (honorific term).

3 Auspicious sight of a holy being, either human or divine.

park. Every night, a large crowd would gather at one part of the extensive courtyard. The scholars who came together gave speeches, followed by a discourse by Śrī Bhagavatpūjyapād Ācāryacaraṇ.

The scholars were of a very high standard. Their speeches—which covered dharma, devotion, knowledge of detachment, human life and the clear discrimination of its duties—were like the sound of the morning conch dispelling the sleep of illusion. The sharpness of their scholarship, the vigour of their language, and the rhythm of their arguments blended into a clarinet of knowledge. As the morning light spread the people swayed in delight to the tunes of the rhythms.

Group photo with Swami Brahmananda Saraswati at Bandha, near Bheraghat in Jabalpur on Guru Purnima, July 3, 1947. Guru Purnima is the day for honouring one's guru. In this photo, Jugal Kishor Shrivastava is the uniformed guard on the far right.

But when Śrī Ācāryacaraṇ's teaching began it was as if the sun of wisdom arose. Within moments I experienced amazing thoughts and feelings never experienced before. His words were a nectar of divine sound that awakened the soul. They carried the essence of Vedas and scriptures in deep, meaningful, soothing language that was expressed so simply that it could be easily absorbed and accepted without hesitation. The flow of the divine lecture by Guru Dev— delivered with a pleasing fatherly smile—was like the constant, peaceful stream of Mother Ganga river, carrying authoritative, blissful and invigourating wisdom.

I was reminded of my childhood when my revered father would take me on his lap and shower me with enormous love and teach me high values. But this moment was even more wondrous and divine. People who were lost in the jungle of saṃsāra (cycle of birth and death; worldly life) found their way, the helpless found support, light emerged in the darkness and the blind opened their eyes again.

Completely filled with faith and affection, all present performed the pūjā[4] of Mahārājśrī with illumined lamps. The meeting concluded and everyone returned home with their lamps in hand. They had come lost but left awakened. This

4 Ceremonial worship of a guru or deity.

unprecedented event left an indelible impression on my heart.

Each day there was darśan during the day and spiritual instructions in the evening. The devotees taking benefit of this program were overwhelmed with their good fortune. Why had the pious efforts of many lives not brought success before? Simply because for over a hundred and fifty years many generations of people did not even know the location of the shrine of Uttarakhand established by Adi Śaṅkarācārya.[5] In the absence of an authorized saint to preside over that shrine, the prospect of getting darśan and hearing lectures was but a distant dream.

People returning from Badrikāśram would often speak of a dilapidated structure near Badrīdhām that the locals called "Jośīmaṭh." Few knew that this was the principal seat of Jyotiṣpīṭh or Jyotir Maṭh established by Adi Bhagvān Shankarcharya. What is the peculiarity of the four divine seats that he established? What is their merit? What are their essential properties, and what is the authority of the principal leader? For several generations the general public had been unaware

5 Ādi Śaṅkara (788-820 CE), the great sage and most famous exponent of Advaita Vedanta (absolute non-dualism), established four seats of learning in the north, south, east and west of India to propagate his teachings. The northern seat is Jyotir Maṭh in the Himalayas.

of such things. The darkness of ignorance had been dense, the eyes had been shut and people stumbled on life's journey.

Today practically everyone knows that the time of awakening has arrived. The giver of the light of knowledge, the guide on the path of spirituality, the bestower of nectar, the one specialist to correct our vision is among us! The radiance of the torch of knowledge is spreading. The darkness of ignorance is being removed. What does a blind man want? Vision, and the bliss in gaining it. This bliss is to be experienced, not talked about. The entire atmosphere is now permeated with indescribable bliss.

CHAPTER 2

My Initiation at the Lotus Feet

MY first initiation took place according to tradition in the year 1916 at my birthplace in Khuraī, Madhya Pradesh. The guru who gave the mantra was a renowned yogi of noble nature.[6] But in the year 1918 he entered into the state of samādhi (here: dropped his body). I therefore had the benefit of his sacred spiritual instructions for only two years. Moreover, being just a child, I was inattentive and unable to fully understand everything that he taught.

Following my guru's passing, I experienced a constant pain in the heart from the cruel absence. I had the exalted desire to somehow hear the spiritual instructions of Śrī Gurujī again and commit them to memory as best I could. But the golden opportunity for that had already slipped from my hand.

6 In the Indian spiritual tradition, the guru imparts a mantra to the new student at the time of initiation. Mantras are auspicious words, phrases or sounds used in meditation.

For the next quarter of a century—from 1918 to 1942—the yearning of my mind remained unfulfilled. Sometimes, in lonely moments, I felt a glimmering light of hope in a corner of my heart. "Gurujī yogī was a mahātmā (great soul)," I thought, "and seeing my dejected state, maybe he will show mercy on me and somehow provide me darśan and spiritual instruction."

With this thought of the mahātmā in mind, over the next 24, 25 years I kept trying, as best I was able, to take advantage of saintly darśans and satsaṅgs.[7] I had darśans of excellent mahātmās and heard spiritual instructions, but always the mind would say, "Your Gurujī has not come." Many times I thought, "why don't I take initiation from some mahātmā?"

With this thought in mind, I met one mahātmā after another over many years. When I received the auspicious darśan of some mahātmā somewhere, I would sometimes think, "This mahātmā seems to be of high rank and also a great scholar. Shall I take initiation from him? Dattātreya[8] had 24 gurus, I will be satisfied with only two."

Immediately the thought would come, "Guru

7 "Association with saints or sages" or a meeting of devotees to discuss spiritual teachings.

8 A paradigmatic Sannyāsi (monk) and one of the lords of Yoga, venerated as a Hindu god.

Brahmā, Guru Viṣṇuḥ, Guru Devo Maheśvaraḥ." The guru is the incarnate Parabrahman.[9] Will I see him in that way? If the mind does not first properly understand Brahmā, Viṣṇu and Maheśvar, how can it possibly understand the incarnate Parabrahman? And again, if he is indeed a mahātmā, how will the mind conceive of a human being as Parabrahman?

I saw numerous mahātmās in various states—delighted and displeased, in comfort and discomfort, eating and drinking, awake and sleeping, healthy and unhealthy. When compared with Brahmā, Viṣṇu, Maheś and Parabrahman, how could I ever accept them? These thoughts unsettled my mind, disallowing shelter. My condition was like that described in the Rāmāyaṇa, where it is said that "in the initial stages, ignorance causes one to be troubled and confused." In that way, the heartache for my guru left me greatly perplexed.

It was immediately clear that my years of searching had ended when, in that year of 1942, I saw the Lord of the Yogīs Śrī Jyotiṣpīṭhādhīśvar Bhagvān in a procession seated on an elephant. It was as if all the ignorance and wrong reasoning dissolved in the air. My mind rejoiced and firmly proclaimed: "This is He. This is the one who has come to quench my endless thirst and fulfil the longing of my life."

---

9 The Supreme transcendent Being.

On inquiry, I learned from one of the residents of the āśram that Śrī Mahārāj did not give personal initiation to just anyone. Only brahmins versed in the Vedas were able to receive the grace of Mahārāj. Non-brahmins were not permitted to receive initiation. Some of my friends received the same answer when they enquired. Many asked me what should be done. We were confronted with a very vexing problem but were resolved not to give up, thinking "someday the merciful, divine soul will hear our heart's desire."

One morning at about 8 a.m., after I got up from my pūjā, a thought came to my mind: "why don't I personally approach the lotus feet of Śrī and request initiation? Then, whatever the answer, I will abide by it." Joy and excitement arose in my mind. I reached for my bicycle and headed toward Baldev Bāg.

I had only gone a short distance when someone called out from far behind in a weeping voice "Dādā! Dādā!"[10] I slowed down, turned and looked over my shoulder. I caught sight of my friend Rāmnārāyaṇ Śarmā hunched over on his bicycle racing wildly after me shouting, "Dādā, do not leave me, I need your support." Even though it was winter, sweat dripped from his temples and he was breathless.

10 Elder brother in local Indian dialect.

Swami Brahmananda seated on an elephant on the holy occasion of 1000 Kundi Yagna performed in March/April 1943 on the banks of the river Yamuna in Delhi (source: Shri Brijesh Kumar Shrivastava, younger son of author).

Rāmnārāyaṇ Śarmā was a railway employee with chronic dysentery. In his heart he felt himself to be my younger brother. He asked, "Where are you going?" I hadn't told my destination to anyone, even those in my own house. So I said, "Don't worry, I'm not leaving you. I'm just going to the market. You shouldn't be rushing about on your bicycle in your weak condition! Don't you think you should avoid such undue exertion?"

"I don't believe you," he said, still short of breath. "You're not going to any market. And why are we standing here in the street? Don't deprive me of your auspicious company!"

Looking at him I thought, what a clean and pious soul! "Alright," I said, "come along."

When we arrived in Baldev Bāg we asked an assistant paṇḍit for a private interview with Mahārājśrī. The paṇḍit said, "At the moment Śrīcaraṇ is dictating letters. You may have to wait for one or two hours." It was about nine o'clock in the morning and the sunlight felt very pleasant. So we went to the lawn and sat on a bench to wait.

About half past ten I received permission for the private meeting. The rule was that only the person who had obtained permission for the meeting could attend. I stood and entered the private room of Mahārājśrī. I closed the door and was bowing down when suddenly Rāmnārāyaṇ rushed in from the outer room and stood beside me to make an obeisance. Mahārājśrī asked us to close the door and be seated. I sat, but Rāmnarāyaṇ remained standing with his hands and elbows together in obedience.

"Who is he?" Mahārājśrī asked. Respectfully I answered, "Bhagvān! He is a brahmin. His name is Rāmnārāyaṇ Śarmā. He comes from Bhopāl and works in the railway department. He is my younger brother, not by birth but by way of the heart."

"Sit down," Mahārājśrī said, shaking gently with laughter. "Tell me," He said, "what's the news?" I can't begin to describe how much interest, parental affection and assurance filled Mahārājśrī's eyes.

I answered by telling Mahārājśrī in summary about my first initiation in 1916, and how my guru took samādhi (left his body) two years later. I told Him the long story of my distress in searching for a guru. I beseeched Mahārājśrī to re-initiate me, if the scriptures permitted. I explained that an assistant in the āśram told me that Śrī Mahārāj only gives initiation to brahmins versed in the Vedas. I said if this were so, I would abide by whatever he instructed.

Several books and other items were sitting on a teapoy near Śrīcaraṇ's seat. Mahārājśrī said, "Hand me the pañcāṅg[11] from there." I placed the

11 A booklet containing daily planetary constellations.

pañcāṅg in the lotus hands of Mahārājśrī. Śrīcaraṇ looked at it for several moments and then said, "Tomorrow morning from 9 to 11 o'clock there will be a particular planetary alignment and lunar phase resulting in a "sarvārtha siddhi yoga."[12] It is rare that they all coincide. Such an opportunity is considered the best for ordaining renunciates and wandering ascetics. Come tomorrow at that time. Ask śāstrījī (one who knows the traditional rituals) for the material for the pūjā. A re-initiation in this connection is according to the scriptures."

Rāmnārāyaṇ instantly moaned and cried out, "Bhagvān! Have mercy on me, too!" Mahārājśrī looked at him and said with a magnanimous, fatherly smile: "You are already joined with Jugal Kishor! Come tomorrow together with him. All right, now go." How clearly the trikālajña[13] mahātmā was seeing all! We made our obeisances and departed.

There was no limit to our delight! We had been told that it would be impossible to get initiation, but now learned that we would not only be initiated, but that it would be at such an auspicious moment! It was as though an ocean of compassion,

12 An auspicious time to begin something new with the best results.

13 Knowing the three times (i.e., the past, present, and future); omniscient.

kindness, mercy, grace, bliss and peace arose in waves. If the friend of the poor, the sea of mercy, the purifier of the guilty, the one who affords support to the lowest and most unworthy would leave us, then who would save us? Mahārājśrī had not said a word about being a brahmin or not. We learned later that the restriction on initiation to brahmins only applied to the initiation of wandering ascetics.

That evening, a brotherly friend, Guruśaraṇ Lāl Jī Saksenā, came to visit me. He lived in the Bāī kā Bagīcā and was a subdivisional officer in the military engineering service. As soon as he entered he embraced me, burst into tears and said, "Brother, you are blessed, but I am left behind." He stood quietly sobbing. Consoling him, I said, "Why are you afraid? Your heart's desire will also be fulfilled. Beseech Bhagvān Guru Dev tonight." Guruśaraṇ responded, "Brother, together with you there is some hope, as there was success with Rāmnārāyaṇ! Otherwise there is a rigid restriction. At the present time there is no hope of getting permission." I said, "Don't think like that. Beseech Mahārājśrī for initiation tonight. You will see that there is boundless love and unlimited kindness."

At that time a sacrifice was being performed at the Kālī temple in the main market. Mahārājśrī had been invited to attend. At around 12 o'clock that night, Mahārājśrī returned with his disciples to the āśram at Baladev Bāg. At about 1 o'clock, Guruśaraṇ met Mahārājśrī and he too got the permission for initiation.

The next day, at the auspicious planetary alignment, we three were initiated. Our lives were blessed! We were endowed with abundant bliss. In the powerful protection of Śrīcaraṇ we became free from anxiety. It seemed as if the burden of the sins of many births was removed. I experienced unique bliss, joy and lightheartedness.

Bhagvān in the form of Śrī Kṛṣṇa had said, "sarva dharmān parityajya, māmekam śarṇaṃ vraja. ahaṃ tvā sarva pāpebhyo mokṣayiṣyāmi mā śucaḥ."[14] This became evident to us at once. Worldly people do not have steady faith even in Bhagvān's words. This faith comes only through direct experience!

14 "Abandon all dharmas and come to Me as your sole refuge. I shall liberate you from all sins, have no sorrow." (Bhagavad Gītā, chapter 18, verse 66).

The author, Jugal Kishor Shrivastava, on the day of his initiation by Swami Brahmananda Saraswati in Jabalpur in 1942.

CHAPTER 3

Purity Overcomes Envy

I have explained how my second brotherly devotee, Guruśaraṇ Lāl Jī Saksenā, came to be initiated. Seeing the pure love and the pristine inner self of this friend, I became jealous. Although we were very compatible, my jealousy tainted my love for him. Seeing his unlimited love and faith for Guru Caraṇ, I told Guru Dev on one occasion how I envied him. Guru Dev smiled and said, "What will you do? Everyone has his very own kind of faith."

CHAPTER 4

Guru Dev Graces Bāī kā Bagīcā

SO many reminiscences come to mind now. What shall I write down and what shall I omit? It's a problem. I will choose a few, although it pains me that I am unable to write them all.

Mahārājśrī dwelled for a few days in Prayāg and then, at the end of the summer, returned to Jabalpur and graced Baldev Bāg with His presence. It was decided He would remain there for cāturmās (four months of rainy season).

As soon as the rainy season started, it was discovered that the roof of the building in which Mahārājśrī stayed was leaking. So the camp moved to a building called "Rain Baserā" in the market area. There the program of darśans and spiritual instructions were resumed.

I continually saw that prominent citizens of different neighbourhoods would invite Mahārājśrī to their locality. Many such requests were made to Mahārājśrī. Representatives from different societies and associations would also regularly invite Mahārājśrī to their respective localities. But Mahārājśrī did not go anywhere. He explained this to the aspirants in such a beautiful way that the rejection of their requests did not disappoint them. He would say, "I have already come to your town to give teachings on dharma. I have come a long distance from the Himalayas to here. You at least can walk a few steps to this place. This is only a small inconvenience for you. No harm comes of it. On the contrary, there is much gain. Please think of what you are asking. If you cannot spare even the small time to come here, instead making us come to you, then today we would be called to many different suburbs, and tomorrow we will be asked to go from home to home. This is not appropriate. It is like saying, 'Oh fruit of the banyan tree, fall into my mouth.'"

Apart from going to the Jabalpur for the sacrifice at the Kālī temple in the main market, Mahārāj never went to any suburb. Although I knew that, the thought came to me that the soil of my neighbourhood would become holy if the dust of Śrīcaraṇ's feet would fall there. At the time, I lived in a rented apartment at Bāī kā Bagīcā (Lady's Garden). It was a large old garden that had been divided into plots and sold. About five to ten houses had been built, with more to follow. The garden was surrounded on all sides by a dirty stream of water. Close by, across the road, was a community of the khaṭīks.[15] The pigs they reared used to wander into our area.

I asked myself, how could holy dust have ever fallen here before? If His dust would fall on this soil, then all of us living here would be prosperous and I could regard myself as free from the debt of this soil. Moreover, why would even Adi Bhagvān Śaṅkarācārya have come here in ancient times? With these thoughts in mind I arrived at the āśram in the evening.

Among the scholars who had come together with Mahārājśrī, it appeared that paṇḍit Dvārikāprasād had special influence in the āśram. So I expressed my wish to him. I described the location and characteristics of my neighbourhood and asked for his help in fulfilling my noble wish that Mahārājśrī come visit there.

The paṇḍit was greatly astonished at my request. He asked, "What kind of people are living there?"

"Most are lower class, but a few middle class families have settled there," I said. The paṇḍit, who was rather corpulent, shook his head intensely and angrily said, "Absolutely not! What kind of man are you? Do religious leaders of high order,

15 A caste engaged in rearing pigs. This caste belongs to the *śūdra varṇ* (caste).

the teachers of the dharma, go to any such places? Do you even know the protocol of inviting such saints?"

"My inability and ignorance are abundant," I humbly replied. This made the paṇḍit laugh, but then he firmly said, "No! What you ask is impossible."

I had earlier asked the paṇḍit for a private meeting with Mahārājśrī. When permission came, I stood up, went to the feet of Śrī, made an obeisance, and sat down.

He asked, "Tell me, what is the news?" In one breath I said, "Bhagvān! As I have already communicated before, I live in Bāī kā Bagīcā, the garden at the eastern edge of the town. A new colony is settling there. Previously it was a rough area. People used to be assaulted and robbed in broad daylight. Lower class people are living in the vicinity. Some people from the middle class are now settling there. The place is surrounded in all directions by a dirty stream, and has become a field for pigs, due to the favour of the municipality and the residence of the khaṭīks nearby. The idea came to me that if the dust of Bhagvān Guru Dev's feet would fall there, then that place would become a holy and divine site. Since the earth has been created, has this soil ever received such auspiciousness? If I could be the cause for this virtuous task, then the land will certainly bless me. In short, with this desire I bow down to Śrīcaraṇ's feet."

Mahārājśrī listened with a delighted expression. But I feared that as soon I finished speaking His order would be, "All right, make your obeisance and leave. I will not go there." I expected this because Mahārāj never went even to the abodes of very illustrious people, despite their many requests, so why would He agree to this? Yet the request of an ordinary man without any resources was granted! The Dharmsamrāṭ (Emperor of dharma) instructed, "Tomorrow evening at 8 o'clock will be fine. Arrange for some people from the āśram to arrive beforehand and I will follow."

Overwhelmed with joy I said, "Bhagvān! By your causeless kindness I am immensely grateful. But no one in our group knows how to receive or worship a divine saint, let alone Akhaṇḍbhūmaṇḍalācārya (teacher of the whole world) Dharmsamrāṭ Jagadguru Bhagvān Śaṅkarācārya. The whole program will be flawed due to our ignorance. Please overlook our incapacity and childish actions and forgive us." Mahārājśrī said, "All right. The time is set tomorrow evening at 8 o'clock."

Blessings on Guru Dev! Śrīcaraṇ paid no attention to our ignorance, incapacity, defects, etc. From that moment it was apparent everything was forgiven. After I made my obeisance and left the private room, I felt abundant bliss and walked with a strut. Seeing my happy state, the paṇḍit said, "Sir, what's happening? What did Mahārājśrī say?"

I replied, "In brief, all of you people should be ready tomorrow at 7:30 p.m. Everyone is to go ahead first and Śrīcaraṇ will follow."

"What?" the paṇḍit exclaimed. "Mahārājśrī has given the approval to go to that place? What did you say to Him?"

"I simply described the situation there," I answered. "Now go and get ready."

"Never, never!," he exclaimed. "You must have misunderstood Him. Why should Mahārājśrī go to such a place?" With that he got up and went to the private room of Mahārājśrī and said, "Bhagvān! That place is almost on the outskirts of the town and the inhabitants still aren't properly settled. This gentleman has admitted that the place is bad, and that the people do not know the protocol for receiving Mahārājśrī according to His status. Since Mahārājśrī has not gone anywhere else in this town, it would not be right for Mahārājśrī to go there. Mahārāj should reconsider this. Furthermore, beginning tomorrow other people would start coming one after another to extend invitations to their localities. It will become very burdensome."

In Sāndrānandpayodhi (Ocean of intense bliss) a wave rose and the paṇḍit received the answer in a calm, dignified voice: "I have agreed upon tomorrow evening at 8 o'clock. I am to arrive there at 8 o'clock. All people should get ready beforehand."

Who can ignore the instructions of Bhagvān? The paṇḍit returned. Many people surrounded me and asked all kinds of questions. Paṇḍitjī said, "Sir, you are a very peculiar person. All right, what kind of transport do you have?"

"I have but a single bicycle," I answered, "but surely I will take you there with a lot of respect."

Though the paṇḍit was an excellent scholar, he would sometimes get angry. But he was also an easy-going person. He burst out laughing and said, "All right brother! In whatever manner you arrange, we shall get there. You are a very fortunate person!"

The next day a pandal (pavilion) was erected in a large field in Bāī kā Bagīcā. The area was about one and a half furlongs (about 300 meters) from the crossing of the state highway. Preparations were made to ready the entire area to welcome Mahārājśrī.

By around 7 o'clock in the evening, much of the decorating of the pandal was still not finished. My associates left their offices at 5:00 p.m. and, without stopping for dinner, went directly to work preparing for the auspicious event. They worked busily, bursting with inner happiness. After I completed my evening routine of worship, I went to the site.

I was dismayed to see that much remained to be done. Bunting and stacks of mango leaves for constructing bandanwar (welcome gates) were piled up in front of the pandal. These still had to be tied together. Some gas lanterns had still not arrived. The carpet had not been laid on the pandal and the barrier had not been placed in front of the ladies' seating area.

One gazetted officer wearing a dhoti (a lower garment of linen cloth) was in a mango tree picking leaves for the bandanwar. I scolded him: "You have waited until the last minute to pick mango leaves. When will the bandanwar be finished?" I was very agitated, but the others were brimming with elation and energy. They said to me, "Bhāī Sahib (elder brother), please go to Baldev Bāg and collect Mahārājśrī. We will take care of all the arrangements here."

At this moment a lean young man humbly approached me holding a sheet of paper. He said, "On the occasion of the auspicious arrival of Jagadguru Bhagvān, I have written a short poem. May I please recite it in front of Mahārāj?"

I frowned. Although I was acquainted with the youth, I was surprised by the request. After all, did the boy think this was to be some sort of poetry conference? Would there be a recitation of the Vedic hymns and the boy's poems in front of Jagadguru Bhagvān? But restraining myself I asked, "What poem?"

The youth handed me the paper. After reading just two or three verses I was amazed. During my student life I also used to write poems, articles, stories and so forth, and I tried hard to have these published in papers and magazines. But after reading this emotional poem, I felt endless bliss and pride. I saw in this lean boy a special radiance. Lovingly I said, "Yes, you may recite your poem. It is very beautiful. Stay in this spot. When Mahārājśrī arrives there will be a lot of commotion and it will be difficult to find you if you wander around. So stay right here."

Trucks and cars began to arrive. I took a few of the vehicles with some men and proceeded to Baldev Bāg to collect Mahārājśrī. When the vehicle carrying revered Ācāryacaraṇ arrived at Ghamapur crossing near Bāī kā Bagīcā, it was greeted by a large crowd. The people shouted welcome slogans and sprinkled Mahārājśrī with flowers. Before us, a scout band was playing and scouts surrounded the vehicle carrying Mahārājśrī. At various intervals there were decorated bandanwars. The air was filled with the tinkling of bells and the blast of conch shells. Families holding welcome lamps lined both sides of the road leading to the pandal.

Swami Brahmananda seated on a motor vehicle in a procession in Mussoorie on September 23,1952. Maharishi Mahesh Yogi is the disciple with dark hair and beard seated on the right.

From time to time the car carrying Mahārājśrī stopped and the people performed āratī (worshipping ceremony with a lamp), threw flowers and chanted prayerful slogans. A wonderful serenity and sanctity permeated the atmosphere. The voices of the people were rejoicing, their bodies were enraptured and their eyes were filled with tears of bliss. The scene was truly extraordinary. Just as the armies of a tyrant part on the arrival of a great, brilliant, mighty and spirited emperor, the lifeless centuries-old impurity of this suburb, and the dense darkness of the inmost soul of the local inhabitants, vanished as Mahārāj's car slowly advanced. Indeed, how can the sun and the night live together?

When the procession arrived at Bāī kā Bagīcā, it grew into a large gathering. When Mahārājśrī took his seat on the stage, the people seated themselves at their appropriate places. Eleven paṇḍits performed Śrī Ācāryacaraṇ's pūjā and abhiṣek[16] with Vedic mantras according to the prescribed rituals. Afterwards the aforementioned youth came forward and recited his poem, pouring out his heart at Śrīcaraṇ's feet. The poem had a very profound impact on all listeners, including the scholars.

Śrīcaraṇ (Mahārājśrī) cast a blissful glance at the boy. The effect on the young man was profound. This youth-poet, who had been living with his father, mother and siblings, soon became detached and devoted himself entirely to the service of Mahārājśrī. Later he became known as Śrī Mahesh Jī (Bal Brahmachari). He spent thirteen years in close, devoted service of

16 Consecration, anointing ceremony, ritual bathing.

Śrīcaraṇ. Today the world knows him by the name Bal Brahmachari Maharishi Mahesh Yogi.

After Bhagwan Guru Dev became Brahmalīn[17] Maharishi, per the instruction and guidance of Mahārājśrī, began teaching the knowledge and practice of a simple method of deep meditation around the world. He has circled the globe three times and is continuing at present. Thousands of foreigners from America, Canada, Australia, Germany, Austria, Sweden, etc. have learned this meditation practice with deep interest and confidence. More are learning every day.

Immediately after the poetry reading, scholars delivered very commendable speeches. In the end Śrī caraṇ gave spiritual teachings. The numerous men and women present drank the nectar of these discourses, which they had never tasted before, and they regarded their life as blessed. The gathering concluded with loud shouts of "Victory to Śrī Ācāryacaraṇ." Śrī Ācāryacaraṇ then departed for Baldev Bāg with his group of āśram people.

In the history of the Bāī kā Bagīcā, this day is inscribed in golden letters. It should be recorded, but who shall write of it? Now, about twenty years later, I sit down to write the "Reminiscences of Bhagvān Guru Dev" and describe this place and what occurred there. In the meantime, much has

17 Left his material body, became absorbed in Brahman.

changed. Many in our group have moved away and new people have come. Bāī kā Bagīcā has transformed into a populous and beautiful suburb. People from various provinces of the country, from different classes—the wealthy class, labor class and the middle class—all are now dwelling here.

But how many of them are blessed with the sacred remembrance of that most auspicious holy day? Whatever will be, if these lines of mine remain somewhere in the world, then the stories about this place and about the happiness, peace and the rise of the local inhabitants, and its original low state, will continue to be told. Receiving them makes human life successful.

The influence of this original source is felt not only in the good fortune of this place. It has also provided the world such a special personality who, with the grace of Bhagvān Guru Dev, has risen to high esteem: Bal Brahmachari Maharishi Mahesh Yogi. From him the world is learning not only the lesson of happiness and peace but also the method of transcendental meditation that allows one to experience it immediately. Readers! This writer has ample reason to be proud of this.

The origin of all these blessings is that holy day, when Bhagvān Guru Dev Anantśrī,[18]

18 An epithet of the god Viṣṇu; anant: endless, boundless, infinite, eternal.

adorned Jagadguru Bhagvān Śaṅkarācārya Jyotiṣpīṭhādhīśvar[19] Śrī Swāmī Brahmananda Jī Saraswatī Jī Mahārāj, on the request of this helpless servant, showed compassion to bless this place with Śrīcaraṇ's dust.

19 Adhīśvar– an epithet of Lord Shiva

CHAPTER 5

Guidance on Prāṇāyāma and Āsanas

ONE day I privately asked Bhagvān Guru Dev, "Bhagvān! I practice two to four kinds of prāṇāyāmas (breathing exercises) and ten to fifteen āsanas (yoga postures). Should I continue this practice or stop?"

He said, "Close both doors from the inside." Both doors were bolted from the inside.

"What do you practice?" He asked. I said, "Bhagvān! The usual prāṇāyāmas—bhastrikā,[20] bhrāmarī,[21] śītalī.[22]"

"Good!" He said. "Which āsanas do you do?"

I answered, "Śīrṣāsana (headstand),

20 A breathing exercise which stresses on quick breathing that puts stress on your abdominal muscles.

21 Bhrāmarī is the Sanskrit word for bee, and this prāṇāyāma is so named because of the humming sound produced at the back of the throat during the practice.

22 Śītalī means "cooling" in Sanskrit. To practice śītalī prāṇāyāma, the tongue is rolled and then the breath is drawn in through the tongue as if through a straw. The exercise has a cooling effect.

mayurāsana (peacock posture), paścimottanāsana (back stretched out posture), ardhasarvāṅgāsana (half shoulder stand), sarvāṅgāsana (shoulder stand), padmāsana (lotus posture), baddhapadāsana (bound lotus posture), kukuṭṭāsana (rooster posture), garuḍāsana (eagle posture) and naulī (turning of the abdominal muscles)."

"Wait!" he said. "You have not eaten for the past two or three hours, isn't that so?"

"I have not eaten recently, Mahārāj," I answered.

"Do the naulī exercise," He said.

After lom-vilom[23] I showed the right-sided naulī, the left-sided naulī and the middle naulī.

"You perform it well," He said. "Now make the headstand."

I did that too. Mahārājśrī continued to say the names of āsanas and I continued to perform them. In that way I performed five āsanas.

He then told me to sit down. With a delighted expression, Mahārājśrī Jī said, "You have mastered three or four āsanas almost perfectly." He then asked, "What is the population of this town?"

"It must be around 250,000 to 300,000," I answered.

He said, "For so many people there must be at

23 Alternate nostril breathing exercise is one of the main practices of prāṇāyāma.

least twenty-five to thirty thousand lavatories and five to seven thousand drains?"

"That is true, Bhagvān!" I answered. "It may be even a little more," I humbly suggested.

Mahārājśrī then explained, "From the heat of the sun, these very polluted elements rise to the air and spread. If you practice these various prāṇāyāmas sitting in the town, this contaminated air will fill the lungs, as in the practice of pūrak[24]-kumbhak[25] and so forth. This will cause harm, not well-being. This is why we go to a secluded place in the forest to practice yoga. The atmosphere there is peaceful and the air is pure. Several of the exercises must be learned from the guru, not from reading books. And several should be practiced only while sitting near the guru in the event some problem arises that needs to be corrected quickly. For this reason, stop these practices for now. The air of the cities is not suitable for performing them. At the time of pūjā, some simple prāṇāyāma is alright, but there is no need to do more. All you need to progress is the method of spiritual practices I gave you during initiation. Do those, and increase your practice over time."

---

24 Closing the right nostril and drawing up air through the left nostril.

25 Stopping the breath by shutting the mouth and closing both nostrils with the fingers of the right hand.

"As blissfully commanded, I shall follow," I said. I then bowed and went home. From that day on I suspended the practice of āsanas and prāṇāyāma. In this way I was protected from any foreseen harm by the grace of Bhagvān Guru Dev.

CHAPTER 6

Blessings Silently Bestowed

ONE day I arrived at Baldev Bāg and asked Bhagvān Guru Dev, "Bhagvān! I follow the instructions I received from You during initiation. Before my initiation I kept several pictures and statues of deities at my place of worship. Should I continue worshipping all of them or only my iṣṭa deva (chosen deity)?

From Mahārājśrī's blissful śrīmukh[26] the nectar of grace poured forth. He said, "It is fine, keep your shop decorated. This will indeed help you. The iṣṭa deva is to be kept secret. It should not be announced publicly. When there are several deities displayed, no one will know which is your iṣṭa. It is good to worship them all. Whatever instructions are given during initiation carry them out strictly.

"You should always remember that apart from your iṣṭa there is nothing to be worshiped in the world. Wherever, whichever, whosoever is worshipped, know that what is worshipped is only your iṣṭa in different form. By strengthening this

26 Face or mouth of Viṣṇu, honorific term.

conviction, feelings of enmity and opposition towards other religions or religious sects will vanish. All will appear as worshippers of different forms of your own iṣṭa. Then there will remain no passion and aversion with anyone. In that way you strengthen your iṣṭa. You should not weaken the iṣṭa.

"Suppose you adore Bhagvān Rām as your iṣṭa and do not believe in Bhagvān Kṛiṣṇa. If you subtract from the form of Śrī Rām one of Bhagvān's forms, the form of Śrī Kṛiṣṇa, do you strengthen or reduce your iṣṭa? In the same way, if you regard Bhagvān Kṛiṣṇa as your iṣṭa, then by subtracting Bhagvān Rām from him, how is your iṣṭa strengthened? After depriving your iṣṭa of such a great form, your iṣṭa is weakened. Think in the same way regarding Bhagvān Śaṅkar (Lord Śiva), Devī Durgā, Gaṇeś and so forth. Not only in your country of sanātana dharma (eternal dharma), whenever somebody's worship is being done anywhere in the world, it is just the worship of your iṣṭa in various names and forms. With this understanding, you will remove attachment and aversion from your heart, a wonderful feeling of bliss will emerge and your vision will be expanded.

"People do not understand this practice. It is ananya bhakti (unique exclusive devotion). No one except your iṣṭa is being worshipped. If you take this perspective towards followers of different religions and worshippers of God throughout the world, you will develop love towards them."

I humbly submitted, "Bhagvān! But the followers of different religions do not think like that. They feel malice towards us, true?"

"That may be," Guru Dev replied, "but the corrupted behaviour of others should not be imitated. One should do only what the Vedic scriptures prescribe and what gurus instruct. When seeing someone else drinking alcohol, the wise man, believing in the Vedic scriptures, will not abandon the water of the Ganges and drink alcohol. The drunkard surely will suffer the consequences of his actions."

I said, "Bhagvān! I study different scriptures, should I continue doing so, or should I study a particular text?"

Mahārāj replied, "Continue the pūjā-pāṭh[27] that you have been doing. You already had railway coaches. Now I have attached a locomotive. However fast you run the engine, the entire train will run at the same speed. Keep the engine running and you will surely reach the destination."

Now my bliss became limitless. Such bliss is the true blessing and grace of Mahārājśrī.

How many people tried to receive Śrīmukh's

27 Worship with recitation of religious texts.

verbal blessings? Mahārājśrī would bestow favour to everyone, but having gained vāk siddhi,[28] Mahārājśrī did not have to express it in words. Whatever lengthy prostration people might make, Mahārājśrī' would just watch silently. Mahārājśrī must have been giving blessings silently, but not in spoken words. Sometimes, however, when people prostrated, He would gently say "Nārāyaṇ."

Once Śrīcaraṇ said that blessings were not bestowed as cheaply here as He had seen in the princely state Rīvā several years before. There, on seeing a ṭhākur,[29]zamīndār[30] or king sitting, blessings were bestowed on people even before they uttered praṇām (respectful greetings), pāylagan (longing for touching the feet) and so forth. Although these people would praise the Brahmins with words like "long live," "always win," "the master!," "food provider!," "long live kingdom!," many were not paying true respect.

Blessings cannot be purchased. Mahārājśrī did not accept money in any form. In Mahārājśrī's camp, signs were hung to inform those coming for darśan that read: "Please do not donate any

---

28 Vāk siddhi is one of the siddhis, or accomplishments, that yogis attain through spiritual practice. Vāk means speech or voice. Vāk Siddhi is the ability to make true whatever is spoken.

29 A person of rank and position, a chief or lord.

30 Landlord.

money here." That meant offerings should be made only by the heart. For those without emotion there was a dearth of benefit. But, as beautiful as the emotion was—excellent, more excellent, most excellent—the reward is proportionate. About this there is not the slightest doubt. The blessings come not through speech, but through silence. I saw this daily.

CHAPTER 7

The Resolution of Problems

IN Bāī kā Bagīcā, ten to twelve of us used to come together regularly for a satsaṅg discussions. Sometimes more friends came. Since Mahārājśrī arrived in town, this close circle began to gather daily to hear His spiritual discourses. We reflected on what we heard and discussed it in our next meeting.

Every evening at 8 o'clock, after our household tasks were completed, we would set off together to attend the divine discourses. On the way, we discussed the remarkable fact that whenever any of us had a question or topic that concerned us, the answer or explanation was always given by Mahārājśrī in the next discourse. And, quite amazingly, the doubts and problems of different people would be resolved simultaneously.

One day when we went off to hear the divine discourses, one of our friends in the neighbourhood said, "Bābūjī![31] You are senior to me. Please forgive my ignorance. I do not understand the

31 Title of respectful address; father.

subjects of faith, trust, bhakti and trikālajñatā discussed by your group. Why is this? These things all seem to me to be imaginary. Sometimes I even laugh about these things, but at other times I feel irritated with myself. What can I do? My education has taken place in such an atmosphere. I have a B.A. degree and worked for many years for the government. I met all kinds of people, good and bad, but I do not believe at all in these spiritual or religious matters. Every Saturday you people study, discuss and lecture. Although I attend these gatherings, I pay no attention and often get sleepy. When you recite Rāmāyaṇ, you all close your eyes, clap and sing:

> Chief of the house of Raghu,
> Lord Rāma, Uplifters of those who
> have fallen, Sītā and Rāma.Victory
> to Raghunandan, victory to Sītā and
> Rāma, daughter of Janaka, be-
> loved Sītā and Rāma.

"Some of you even begin to sway. How can I explain my impudence? I spontaneously break into laughter. I think, what is all this? They make noise, but for what purpose? Bābūjī! I am describing my faithless condition. I hide nothing from you. Please do not be angry."

"Don't worry," I said. "I've known for some time

what you've told me. Go on. You've raised a very good topic. Tell me further what's on your mind."

He replied, "Bābūjī, allow me to go with you to hear Mahārāj's discourses, nothing more."

I encouraged him to explain further. "Bābūjī," he said, "ever since Mahārāj arrived I have been hearing that He is trikāldarśī[32] and antaryāmī.[33] In short, I'd like to learn more about this."

"What?" I said. "You want to know whether Mahārāj is trikāljñaand antaryāmī?"

He replied, "Bābūjī, I know it is sheer stupidity to entertain doubt about such a high mahātmā. . . ."

I interrupted him and said, "Well! Listen! "Hāth kangan ko ārsī kya?" (a Hindi proverb meaning "you don't need a mirror to see the beauty of a bracelet," i.e., facts that are self-evident). You can have your doubts removed today. Think of any topic, question and doubt that you consider appropriate. Then make the sincere, mental request that this be addressed by Mahārājśrī in the next lecture."

"Alright! It's done," he said.

"Whatever you have thought, tell it only to one of our group, whomever you choose," I said. "If Mahārājśrī addresses this subject, even your faithless mind cannot deny it."

---

32 Seeing the three times: past, present and future.

33 One who knows the inmost being of man, all-knowing one.

"I will tell you the subject," he said. He then confided a problem to me and asked that I keep it a secret. The matter was a personal family problem that is quite common. I assured him I would keep the matter to myself.

Finally, we proceeded to Baldev Bāg. This gentleman was my neighbour. He was a graduate and a central government employee. He was from Mirjāpur, Uttar Pradesh, and was a simple and pure hearted person. It was just that his spiritual and religious thoughts were in confusion.

When we reached Baldev Bāg, we found hundreds of people seated on the northwest lawn listening to a lecture by Mahārājśrī. We crossed the street and stood behind where the people were seated. We were about 150 feet from the dais of Mahārājśrī, but could hear the lecture clearly over a loudspeaker.

I said to my neighbour, "Let's sit here, far from the dais. That way you won't think that any of us have disclosed your subject to anyone. Such a great Saint does not need to have this information conveyed by letter or word. Watch us if you want, but pay attention to the lecture."

He gently responded, "Bābūjī! I am your child. Don't you also feel that is so? I have faith and trust in you. It is due to my ignorance that I do not understand the talk about trikāljñaand antaryāmī of the mahātmās. I have openly confessed my ignorance to you."

"Fine," I said, "now pay attention to the discourse."

"I am listening, Bābūjī," he replied. "Please forgive me, but if the topic of my problem is not covered in the discourse, what then?"

"Then tomorrow morning I will sign up to join your sect," I joked, laughing. This gentleman was a follower of a specific religious community.

"No, no Bābūjī," he said, "this was not what I meant, I. . ."

"Look," I interrupted, "Bhagvān Guru Dev will surely keep my faith secure, there is absolutely no doubt about this. So I won't need to fill out any form of your sect. But if Mahārājśrī addresses your subject and your problem is resolved, promise me that you will recite Rāmcaritmānas every day for the rest of your life." He agreed, and I said, "Ok, now let's listen."

The discourse delved deeply into the Veda. Yet Mahārājśrī explained it in a very beautiful and straightforward manner. The gentleman's problem was hundreds of miles away from the subject of the lecture. Five, ten, fifteen minutes passed and the discourse remained only on the subject of the Veda. There was no connection to the problem of the gentleman. The audience listened to the discourse attentively. Then, suddenly, the subject of the discourse shifted. Mahārājśrī said, "All this is on the sphere of paramārtha (highest goal of human life). In the same way, with respect to mundane worldly problems, the śruti,[34] smṛti[35] and purāṇa[36] instruct us about our duties. The ṛṣis (Vedic seers) and munis (saints, ascetics) have also praised the path of the worldly life. Yet out of ignorance and neglect people have become blind with selfishness, doing as they wish and going astray. Their path gets corrupted. In this way, they spoil both this world and the world beyond."

Mahārājśrī continued, "Suppose somebody is troubled by these circumstances… (at which point he described the gentleman's exact problem). He becomes unhappy and disappointed. But the problem will not be solved if one remains sad and uncertain what to do. In such circumstances, follow the path of puruṣārtha[37] according to the scriptures. Manu teaches that at such times you

---

34 The revelation of the Veda which was heard.

35 The body of sacred and profane Brahmanical tradition as "remembered" by men, as distinct from the "revealed" knowledge of the Vedas.

36 Holy scriptures in Sanskrit dealing with all aspects of ancient Indian history, legend, mythology and theology.

37 The four proper goals or aims of a human life: dharma (righteousness, moral values), artha (prosperity), kāma (pleasure, love) and mokṣa (liberation).

must act with courage according to the scriptures and then you will become happy."

Mahārājśrī clearly and precisely described my friend's topic of concern and prescribed the solution. My neighbour was thoroughly amazed. He agreed that Mahārājśrī had addressed the very problem troubling him. The joy we all felt knew no bounds.

After the discourse we returned home. The gentleman said, "Bābūjī, what a strange and wonderful experience! Now, there is no room for any more doubt. This was exactly my private, vexing problem, and now I have its solution. But how exactly am I to apply this guidance? Please shed light on this. Then tomorrow help me purchase a copy of Rāmcaritmānas. I promise to recite it every day of my life."

Not long after the gentleman had the opportunity to ask Mahārājśrī in private how he was to apply what Mahārājśrī had said. His problem was soon resolved per the instructions of Mahārājśrī. That gentleman, Shri Premchand Asthanajī, continues his daily recital of Rāmcaritmānas to this day. In 1948, he was transferred to Prayāg (Allahabad), where he now lives.

In this way we have several times experienced Śri Bhagavatpūñjyapād's[38] trikāljñatā (knowl-

38 "The venerable feet of the Supreme Being."

edge of the three times) and antaryāmitva (all knowingness).

CHAPTER 8

Faith in the Face of Danger

IN the same year of 1942, the camp of Mahārājśrī moved to a building named "Rain Baserā" to the west of Gol Bāzār due to shortage of space in the Baldev Bāg building. At that time, the nationwide movement against the foreign government was at its height. The commotion of the times could be felt in the atmosphere of Jabalpur.

One day, the situation took a violent turn. There was a huge procession in the city in support of the Quit India Movement.[39] At Favvārā, which is in the middle of the market, the police stopped the procession and ordered the protesters to disperse. When they refused, the police charged them and began beating them with canes. The crowd responded by throwing stones at the police vans. Many people on both sides were injured.

Those of us living in Bāī kā Bagīcā heard of these disturbances, but we paid little mind as

39 The Quit India Movement was a movement launched at the Bombay session of the All-India Congress Committee by Mahātmā Gāndhī on August 8, 1942, demanding an end to British rule in India.

such clashes had become common. At about 8:00 p.m., after the evening meal, our group of 8-10 people left Bāī kā Bagīcā to have the darśan of Mahārājśrī. We passed through Sarafa Bazaar, Kamania Phatak, Fawara and Gadha-Phatak to Rain Baserā. It was pitch dark because the electrical wires had been cut.

As we approached Kamania Phatak, we had difficulty proceeding in the dark because the road was covered with rubble and telephone wires. We would trip on the stones and get tangled in the wires. We held hands and carefully moved forward, propelled by our desire to receive the darśan of Mahārājśrī. The darkness, stones and the spider-web of wires did not deter us. If one remains steadfast in the resolve to obtain a sadguru (true guru), this is achieved no matter how many obstacles appear.

Upon reaching Rain Baserā, we received our regular dārśan of Mahārājśrī, along with other guests, and then listened to His spiritual instructions. The news of the turbulence in city had already reached Mahārājśrī. It had begun to rain, so we were able to sit longer at Śrīcaraṇ's feet. At around 11 o'clock, we headed home. We did not know the current situation in the city, but Mahārājśrī gave us permission to leave. He said,

"It is late, and you have far to go. The situation is different today, but have no fear. Now go."

The 8 p.m. curfew had already been enforced in the city. An American military contingent had been deployed in the city, especially in the market and other major locations. In those days there were many American soldiers in the city.

Talking among ourselves, we progressed from the vicinity of the Baṛā Mahāvīr Jī temple (temple of Lord Hanuman) toward Favvārā, which was just a few steps away. We opened our umbrellas, and the rain made a crackling sound as it fell on them. At that very moment, and in the dense darkness, we heard a voice on our left shouting "Hey! Hey!" The voice seemed to be coming closer. At first, we thought there were beggars calling for alms. But then a beam of light suddenly flashed on us and we found ourselves surrounded by soldiers with guns.

At first we thought these were Japanese soldiers who had parachuted into the city. In those days there were often rumours of a Japanese attack. Sometimes there would be radio announcements telling the residents of Jabalpur to relocate 4-5 miles outside the city, as there was a munitions factory in the city that the authorities thought the Japanese might bomb. We thought the Japanese had suddenly arrived by parachute, but soon realised that the soldiers were Americans. Still, we were startled to find ourselves suddenly and unexpectedly confronted with rifles.

One of the soldiers approached us. He seemed to be an officer by his speech and manner. I explained in English from where we had come and why we were out so late. I said that we were government employees, lawyers, doctors and so forth, all of a respectable class of society. I explained that we went out in these dire circumstances and dense darkness due to an important obligation.

The soldier flashed his light on the others in our group. Satisfied, he said, "Look, the government has issued an order to shoot on sight after curfew. If one of our soldiers had shot, you would have been killed. All right! Now go straight (pointing towards Kamāniyā Gate) and don't look back, otherwise you will endanger your life!"

Some of our group started moving forward, but others were speechless and stiff as wood. "Come on," I said, but some remained frozen. I repeated my order and they finally started to move. After we walked some distance, they breathed a sigh of relief and said, "Bābūjī, we could have made our children anāth[40] today, because we easily could have become the victims of the bullets of these foreign soldiers." I said, "The one who is the nāth[41]

---

40 Orphans.

41 Lord, protector, master.

of us all, as long as He, Bhagvān Guru Dev, is with us, nobody is anāth or distressed. The one who protects is greater than the one who kills. What more proof do you need? It is a matter of faith and trust. We had set out to return home with the trust in Mahārājśrī's words: 'The situation is different today, but remain fearless, go!' We have already surrendered ourselves to the shelter of Bhagvān Guru Dev. 'Prabhu sak tribhuvan māri jiāī'[42] (Bhagvān Rām can kill all and bring back to life in the three worlds). The richly bestowed embodiment of saccidānanda (pure absolute being, by nature existence, consciousness and bliss), Bhagvān Guru Dev, told us to remain fearless. If we surrender to fear, would this not be a lack of trust?"

Talking like that we arrived at Bāī kā Bagīcā. On the way, our fellow disciples departed at their crossings: Sarrāfa, Galgalā, Ghamāpur and so forth. Our adventure that night was like none other, and our devotion and faith to Śrīcaraṇ's feet were strengthened and expanded.

42 Quote from the Rāmcaritmānas.

CHAPTER 9

The Root of Mokṣa

THE inhabitants of Jabalpur derived a special grace from the presence of Bhagvān Guru Dev. Ācāryacaraṇ[43] often used to say, "By being inhabitants at the bank of the Narmadā—the giver of siddhi[44]—the minds of you people are naturally in harmony with dharma. If you continue with your practice, the highest welfare will result."

I had a long-standing thirst in my mind for tasting the nectar of Bhagvān Guru Dev's biography. I wanted to learn all the heart-rendering, inspirational, knowledge-filled and immortal episodes of His past. A few drops of His chaste life satisfied my mind like a Chatak bird is satisfied by rain of "Swati Nakshatra." (In Indian mythology and literature "Chatak" is described as a rare bird that remains thirsty for months and only becomes satisfied when particular rains fall when the constellation Svati Nakshatra is aligned at a particular position).

---

43 "Teacher's or guru's feet," an honorific term.

44 Accomplishment, fulfilment, perfection, complete attainment.

Therefore, whenever some saint or elder devotee of Mahārājśrī arrived in the āśram, I would engage them in conversation and ask probing questions. Sometimes I would ask with curiosity about some secret essence of His life. In answering, they would become fully absorbed and speak in an unbroken stream. I beseeched them to tell me stories of the life of Mahārājśrī. Those stories are so beautiful and delightful. They cause the bird of doubt to fly away and bring the highest welfare. On hearing my request, the speaker, who had been speaking affectionately up to that point, would suddenly become subdued and serious. "Babu!" he would say, "Mahārājśrī has not given permission for us to tell you of these things. If we told you these stories, He might order us to say nothing. All right! Now go and visit some religious places."

I would say in reply, "But Mahārājśrī is staying on the upper floor. You can tell me without worry."

He would say, "Babu! Mahārājśrī is Omniscient."

One of the long-standing servants of Mahārājśrī was paṇḍit Īśvardatta Śukla, who was very knowledgeable about astrology. I often used to ask him about his recollections of Mahārājśrī's earlier days. During those conversations I learned that he was very fond of lemons and papayas. I now had an effective weapon! Due to my employment in the Railway Department, I had access to these fruits, even when they were not available in the market. I used to bring lemons and papayas with me and say to the jyotiśjī:

"Jyotiśjī, how would you like it if your meal today included lemons and perhaps also papayas?"

Exhilarated he would say, "Oh splendid, brother! What a question! All things are available in the world, but nothing compares to lemons and papayas." He rejoiced and looked at me with great expectation. The mere mention of lemon and papaya delighted him greatly.

In these moments of great delight he would sing songs of praise to the grandeur of Mahārājśrī's past life. My long-cherished expectations were fulfilled and within view. I wish to impart the treasure of some of these eternally memorable stories and, in that way, pay my gratitude.

The next day we did not find the jyotiśjī in the āśram. I learned that he departed the night before on Mahārājśrī's order.

Recalling his early days with Guru Dev, jyotiśjī used to say, "In our heart the desire for Mahārājśrī's darśan was always burning. In those days Guru Dev dwelled for years in thick deep forest. Disciples, philosophical aspirants and devotees desired Mahārājśrī's darśan and used to perform various religious rituals to obtain it. Some fortunate ones would sometimes receive Mahārājśrī's darśan. It is not like today, when you can come to the āśram and get darśan whenever you wish. This kind of situation did not exist. Bhagvān Guru Dev's unlimited grace is on you people. He who has left the caves of the Himalayas and emerged from the inaccessible forests gives you darśan. He allows you all to drink the nectar of his reviving speech every day. Brother, where was such an opportunity in those days?

Jyotiśjī continued, "Do not consider it as self-praise, but I used to wander from one forest to another for months seeking darśan. Often I returned disappointed, but several times, by the grace of Bhagvān Guru Dev, I obtained His darśan and became contented. On several occasions I sat in a tree pretending to rest in the night. When the Sun God, riding his chariot, rose in the east early in the morning for his journey, I would have Bhagvān Guru Dev's darśan in some cave or under a tree. I was thoroughly spell-bound. I would shout, "Bhagvān! I want to come for your darśan, but the vanrāja (king of the jungle, i.e., tigers or lions) are seated on the path waiting for me. Pūjyapād[45] without your grace how shall I reach there?"

"Our situation was much like that of a pitiful jīva (individual soul) fallen into the cycle of birth and rebirth, whom the ṣadvikār (six enemies of

45 "Whose feet are to be revered," an honorific term.

the soul)[46] are intent to pursue as prey. Even when one is on the path prescribed by the guru, these enemies seek to cause fear or cause the jīva to scare himself. Hearing my talk, Bhagvān Guru Dev would laugh heartily, and then say to the tigers, 'Alright, it's fine, you can go now.' In amazement I would watch both tigers yawn, stretch their limbs and wander off into the dense forest. Still frightened and trembling, I would approach Guru Dev.

46 In Hindu theology, there are the six passions of the mind, which are: kāma (lust), krodha (anger), lobha (greed), moha (delusion), mada (pride), and mātsarya (jealousy), the negative characteristics of which prevent man from attaining mokṣa (liberation, salvation).

"He who, through the shelter of his lotus feet, can disarm even a tiger of its natural violent tendencies, if we do not surrender our bag of vices and the black money bestowed by the six enemies, what will be our misfortune or bad deed? Is this our misfortune or mahāpāpa (heinous sin)? This question is very much worth considering. Verily, we should surrender completely at the feet of Bhagvān Guru Dev. We should put our trust completely on Śrīcaraṇ's grace and capabilities. Then all welfare is possible for us."

Then the jyotiśjī, overwhelmed and with tearful eyes, told us more stories that made us spellbound and fully attentive.

> "The root of meditation is the form of the guru;
> The root of pūjā (worship) is the feet of the guru;
> The root of the mantra is the speech of the guru;
> The root of mokṣa (liberation) is the grace of the guru." (Famous quote from Guru Gita.)

CHAPTER 10

A Message Delivered

IN the year 1944, Jagadguru Śaṅkarācārya Swami Brahmananda Saraswati, the Mahārāj of Jyotir Maṭh, presided over an historical event—the "Śatmukh Koṭi Homātmak" mahāyajña (great sacrifice with 100 fire pits and with the chanting of ten million devotional mantras). After that, Mahārājśrī set up the camp at Bhagīrath Palace (Delhi). At the same time, the convention of the Ārya Samāj had also been organised in Delhi. The chairmanship of the convention had been entrusted to Śrī Śyāmā Prasād Mukharjī.

The organisers of Ārya Samāj sent a series of questions regarding the Vedic Sanātana Dharma to the camp of Jagadguru Śaṅkarācārya Mahārājśrī with the request that appropriate answers be provided to the plenary session the same day. Mahārājśrī directed that the answers be precisely and systematically written down by paṇḍit Śāstrī[47] Benī Mādhava Śukl, who was a

47 One versed in the śāstras (holy scriptures).

Śāstrārth,[48] Mahārathī[49] and Āśukavi.[50] He personally went to the convention to take these papers to the huge procession of Ārya Samāj in order to deliver them to the general secretary of the Ārya Samāj.

Mahāyajña in Delhi in 1944, as seen in a photo published in *Life* magazine.

When he arrived, the volunteers of the procession would not allow him to meet the general secretary while the procession was in progress.

---

48 One versed in the interpretation of a śāstra; a doctrinal debate, discussion; specif. debate between an Ārya Samājī and a sanātan Hindu or a Vaiṣṇava.

49 "Having a great chariot": a great warrior; prestigious person.

50 Extempore poet.

Śāstrārth Mahārathī Śāstrī was desperate and returned to the Bhagīrath Palace and began to consider other ways to deliver the papers to some office bearer of the Ārya Samāj. An idea suddenly came to his despairing mind. He walked over to a part of the camp where some disciples of Guru Dev were engaged in satsang and said, "Is there anyone among the disciples who is a Kāyastha (member of a writing caste)." The people pointed towards me and said, "Yes, Babu, Shri Jugal Kishor Shrivastavajī is an ardent devotee of Guru Dev and a Kayastha as well."

Śāstrārth Mahārathī then told me the whole story. I began to reflect on how I might quickly accomplish this task. Keeping Guru Dev's adorable image in my mind, I said to the others, "Give the papers to me. I will go. Prepare an envelope addressed to "Śrī Śyāmā Prasād Mukharjī, chairman, Ārya Samāj plenary session, New Delhi."

A fellow disciple brought an envelope and addressed it as instructed. The papers were then inserted and the envelope sealed.

I began to think that our Guru Dev is a trikāljña Mahātmā. Keeping the divine image of Guru Dev in my mind, I set off in the direction of the procession. While walking along side the procession, I asked a volunteer, "Is the general secretary or any secretary of the Ārya Samāj present?"

He said that Śrī Śyāmā Prasād Mukharjī was riding on an elephant, and that the general secretary and other office bearers were walking along side. When I asked the volunteer the name of the general secretary, he told me his name. As I continued walking with the procession I said to another volunteer, "I need to meet the general secretary to give him some extremely urgent and important information."

The volunteers were carrying sticks and formed a barrier around the elephant. But hearing my request they lifted the sticks and allowed me to enter the circle. Pointing, the volunteer said "That is the general secretary walking beside the elephant."

In my heart I entreated Guru Dev, "You have transmitted to me an order, therefore, oh Bhagvān, show me such grace that I can accomplish this task successfully."

I caught up with the general secretary and said, "This letter has been sent from Jagadguru Śaṅkarācārya Swami Brahmananda Saraswati Mahārājśrī to the chairman of the convention." He signaled to the elephant-driver to give the letter at once to Śrī Mukharjī and moved on. The elephant-driver signaled the elephant to lower his trunk and I deposited the letter, along with two rupees. Śāstrārth Mahārathī watched as this happened. Śrī Mukharjī opened the letter and began to read it. Śāstrārth Mahārathī saw this too. Upon my return he said, "I knew this work could only be done by a Kāyastha."

After the paṇḍit left, a fellow disciple asked me, "Bābūjī! Why did he entrust this work to a Kāyastha?" I responded, "You people did not understand the real meaning. It has nothing to do with caste. This has nothing to do with Kāyastha caste. Literally the meaning of Kāyastha is 'Kāya' (body) and 'stha' (present). What is present in your body is ātmā (inner soul). Thus, Kāyastha means one who is always attached to his ātmā by words, thought and deeds. Only one who keeps Guru Dev residing in his soul is a true Kāyastha. They are fully surrendered to lotus feet of Guru Dev and are called 'Gurumukh-Nihal' (being always face to face with the guru). I took this task as directive of Guru Dev and it was Guru Dev's līlā (play). In this way the work was accomplished."

Several people have said that the letter I took did not come from Śāstrārth Mahārathī but from paṇḍit Dvārkā Prasād Śāstrī. It doesn't matter either way. The task was completed according to Guru Dev's wish. That is all that matters.

CHAPTER 11

Others First

MAHĀRĀJŚRĪ had been entreated to give His patronage to a very special "Śatmukh Koṭi Homātmak" Mahāyajña (great Vedic sacrifice). The Śaṅkarācāryas of the three other pīṭh[51] had arrived in Delhi for this occasion. Coinciding with this Mahāyajña were huge festivals of the plenary session of the Dharm-Saṅgh (a national religious organisation), as well as a special convention of the Varṇāśram Svarājya Saṅgh (a gathering on cow protection).

As part of these celebrations, there was to be a procession of the Śaṅkarācāryas of the four pīṭh ending at the venue of the special session on cow protection, which the Śaṅkarācāryas were to bless with their august presence.

In the presence of Mahārājśrī, there was some discussion as to which of the Śaṅkarācārya's processions should be first, and in what order the others should follow. One person suggested that

51 Principal seat of a religion; here it refers to the four pīṭh established by Adi Śaṅkarācārya.

it would be appropriate that the Śaṅkarācārya of Jyotir Maṭh go first, with the processions of the other Śaṅkarācāryas to follow, since the Mahāyajña and the convention were being held under the patronage of Mahārājśrī. Very learned paṇḍits and sannyāsī[52] submitted their respective opinions. I was also present in that circle of the Mahārājśrī's disciples. I stood up and said, "Mahārājśrī! Delhi falls under the jurisdiction of the Jyotiṣpīṭh (the northern seat established by Adi Śaṅkarācārya), as everyone knows. Because the Śaṅkarācāryas of the other three pīṭh are our guests, their processions should go first, followed by the procession of Mahārājśrī." Mahārājśrī looked at me smilingly and agreed. I was overwhelmed that Mahārājśrī appreciated my suggestion and deemed it appropriate.

52 One who has abandoned all worldly possessions and affections, an ascetic.

CHAPTER 12

Nothing is Impossible

IN January of 1942, the famous Mahākumbh Melā was organised in Prayāg. Afterwards Mahārājśrī stayed for some days in Kāśī (Varanasi) and then returned for a second time to "Rain Baserā" at Gol Bāzār for the observance of cāturmās.[53] The following year he spent cāturmās in the mansion of the prosperous merchant Rādhākṛṣṇa in Gañjīpurā, Jabalpur.

On these occasions, I had many opportunities to do sevā (service). Several times I performed the night service in the attire of a doorkeeper with a gun. One day I was on duty outside of the room of Mahārājśrī. It was nighttime and very cold. After midnight, Mahārājśrī called from his room, "Jugal Kishor! It is very cold outside, come and sit here."

I obeyed Mahārājśrī's order, entered the room and sat down. Mahārājśrī asked, "Tell me, what is the news?"

Understanding the essence of the question, I

53 Four months stay during the rainy season.

said, "Mahārājśrī, I try to perform my sādhanā[54] according to your instructions, but sometimes my mind roams here and there."

Mahārājśrī replied, "When the mind runs away, then let it run away, don't run after it."

I then said, "Mahārājśrī, may I have, by your grace, the darśan of my iṣṭa deva (chosen god or goddess). This is my first and last wish."

Mahārājśrī replied with a smile, saying, "If you consider your guru as your all and all powerful, then this will very likely happen." He then benevolently imparted to me the method.

Tears fell from my eyes. I became aware of this great blessing. How fortunate is the one who has surrendered completely at Śrīguru's feet and follows the instructions of Śrīguru! For him nothing at all is impossible. This I slowly came to realise.

---

54 Spiritual practices.

CHAPTER 13

The Blessing of My Son at the Feet of Guru Dev

I was initiated by Guru Dev in 1942. Every day I used to meditate and do japa[55] in the manner He instructed. Gradually the mind began to experience bliss.

Mahārājśrī's camp was at Baldev Bāg in Jabalpur. I used to regularly attend the lectures of Mahārājśrī along with other disciples. I would leave my residence at Bāī kā Bagīcā after supper, at around 8:00 p.m., and walk to Baldev Bāg for darśan and the lecture.

As I have already narrated, the thought came to me that I should try to organise a reception for Mahārājśrī at Bāī kā Bagīcā so that the residents could receive the blessings of his august presence. I have detailed this episode in an earlier chapter of this book. When Mahārājśrī's procession approached our Bāī kā Bagīcā neighbourhood, my eldest son, Umesh Kumar Shrivastava, was then just one and quarter years of age. With Umesh

55 Repetition of mantras.

and me at the site were my mother, wife, an elder daughter, Kumari Vidyavati Shrivastava, and my two brothers.

When the grand procession of Mahārājśrī passed near our house, we all made praṇām and saluted in respect. My wife Śmt. Kalavati Devi Shrivastava and I made sāṣṭāṅg-praṇām (prostrated with eight parts of the body). We then performed our duty by placing our son Umesh Kumar Shrivastava at the lotus feet of revered Guru Dev. The infant got initiation simply by dṛṣṭi-dīkṣā, by a glimpse from Mahārājśrī as he rested at His lotus feet.

All parents should endeavour to place their son or daughter at the lotus feet of a divine saint who is well versed in the Veda and has experienced the nectar of bliss. The initiation of my son by the mere glimpse of Mahārājśrī caused him to develop into pious and virtuous youth who showed respect and obedience to his parents and elders and emerged as a worshipper of Lord Śrī Rām.

CHAPTER 14

The Effects of Karma

ONCE, during the season of cāturmās, Guru Dev's camp was set up in Jabalpur. At that time, my cousin Śrī Jagadīś Prasād Shrivastava's first wife became gravely ill. When the doctor said she had little time to live, my aunt went with me to Mahārājśrī to make a humble submission, saying, "Mahārājśrī! My daughter-in-law ardently serves me. She always follows her husband's commands. She is a true pātivrata (according to Indian mythology a faithful, virtuous and devoted wife who gains divine strength). Mahārājśrī may you show grace, so that she may recover. This is my earnest request."

Mahārājśrī replied, "Mother! Your son and daughter-in-law are my disciples. If the life of your daughter-in-law is only this long, her future is bright nonetheless. It is not fitting for us to interfere with the laws of the Creator or with the suffering brought by destiny. The immediate danger could be removed, but it would be inappropriate to do so. And it will return and cause even more suffering. You must be patient and know that her future life will be extremely glorious due to her virtuous deeds. If she advances to a better life as a result of those deeds, she should not be persuaded to stay here. The Creator could become offended by this, and her demotion and harm might follow."

The venerable aunt came home and said to me, "Bhāīyā (brother)! Mahārājśrī's invaluable speech is true, but I could not understand it fully. Please explain it to me."

I said, "Auntie! In this world the coming and going takes place according to the karma of the individual soul, and that soul has to proceed to some other incarnation. It is like in employment—who will stay, where will they stay and how long will they stay? After the employer reviews the record of his works and his honesty or dishonesty, the employee is given a promotion and sent to a good place; or he is demoted and sent to such a place where every kind of inconvenience exists. When receiving a promotion, the wage is also higher, and various kinds of conveniences are included—like good residence, good atmosphere and the opportunity to do good work. Similarly, if his record is bad, then as a punishment he will be demoted, where the wage is less, without good housing and, due to a debased atmosphere, he must endure various kinds of difficulties.

Similarly, Lord Brahma (one of the aspects of the supreme God) evaluates every being by his actions (karma) and accordingly assigns him the body of human or other creature with all attendant circumstances. In good and high incarnations, man finds a good atmosphere, good conveniences, good ways to work and to contemplate the results, and he gets the inspiration to do good works. On the other hand, one with bad actions in his record gets the life of condemned creatures, suffers helplessly and has a short life span. My younger brother's wife is a woman of a dignified family and is an obedient and devoted wife. There is absolutely no doubt that her future will be prosperous. This is what the trikālajña Mahātmā explained to you."

Aunt listened to my words attentively. Although she had tears in her eyes, she was very consoled because:

> One who doesn't follow the Guru's teaching, he acts confused.
> One loses both worldly and spiritual life and faces imminent death.

I was contemplating Guru Dev's lotus feet as I explained this to auntie and felt as though Guru Dev was speaking through me.

CHAPTER 15

Intensify Your Worship

IN those days, Bhagvān Guru Dev was staying in His āśram "Brahma Nivās" in Alopībāg, Prayāg. My family and I had the opportunity to go there. A few other fellow disciples had also come with their families to get Mahārājśrī's darśan. I was suffering from asthma at that time. While having a mild attack of asthma in Prayāg, I thought I should express my worry to Mahārājśrī. When I went along with my family for Mahārājśrī's darśan, I climbed the stairs. Mahārājśrī was sitting in the upper room. I was breathless after climbing the stairs. I made praṇām (obeisance) and sat down. I then explained my health condition to Mahārājśrī, saying, "Bhagavān! By your grace my family and I are happy. It is said that asthma is cured only with one's last breath (asthma was an incurable disease at those times). My elder daughter is now marriageable. After my father took up residence in heaven, my brothers and younger sister are alone. My mother kept crying in grief over my father and has become blind. She lives with me. I am afraid that just as my father left behind sons and a marriageable daughter, I may have the same fate.

Mahārājśrī listened attentively to my anxiety. Gracefully he just said, "Intensify your bhajan."[56]

I carried out His instruction literally. Over the course of time, my daughter married into a good family and is happy. Today, as I write these reminiscences, one of my sons, Ch. Brijesh Kumār Shrivastava, is already holding a post in B.H.E.L (Bharat Heavy Electrical Limited) in Bhopāl. My other son, Umesh Kumar Shrivastava, is studying for his Master of Commerce degree. I believe that all problems are getting solved by the divine grace of Sadguru.

56 Devotional singing in praise of the Divine; more generally, worship.

CHAPTER 16

The Strength to Pass Through Suffering

ONCE Mahārājśrī took a seat in the Miśra Bandhu office in Dīkṣitpurā, Jabalpur. The whole circle of my friends used to go there every day for His darśan. Once I suffered a severe asthma attack. I was out of breath and could not go that day. The next day, when my condition seemed to be somewhat better, I went for Mahārājśrī's darśan together with a group of disciples.

On the previous day, due to increased pain, I had been deprived of hearing Mahārājśrī's divine life-giving words, which I very much regretted. If the body does not cooperate, the patient is helpless. The next day I sat downstairs in the garden of the āśram listening to Mahārājśrī's divine spiritual instructions through a loudspeaker nearby.

Following Mahārājśrī's discourse, after an interval of about one hour, the sequence of his darśans began. People went for Mahārājśrī's darśan, made praṇām (obeisance) and went home delighted.

Śrī Guruśaraṇ Lāl Saksenā, our fellow

disciple from Bāī kā Bagīcā, also went for darśan. Mahārājśrī asked, "Has Jugal Kishor not come today, like yesterday? He usually comes every day."

Śrī Saksenā, a sub divisional officer in M.E.S. (Military Engineering Services) who held me in high esteem and always felt affection for me, said, "Bhagvān! Bābūjī suffered a severe asthma attack yesterday. He had to remain sitting up all night. His body was not cooperative and therefore he could not come yesterday. Feeling somewhat better he managed to come today and is now sitting downstairs. It is my request that you cure him fully of this malady."

Also in the service of the lotus feet of Guru Dev was Brahmachari Mahesh Jī from Bāī kā Bagīcā, Jabalpur (M.P.). Later, when known as Maharishi Mahesh Yogi, he would distribute as a blessing to the world the famous, simple technique of deep meditation, according to the instruction of Mahārājśrī. He has been propagating this meditation technique in many countries around the globe. People have therefore been able to learn the simple technique of deep meditation known as bhāvātīt dhyān (transcendental meditation).

Śrī Saksenā said to Brahmachari Śrī Mahesh, "Please arrange for Bābūjī to have Mahārājśrī's darśan in privacy. Though the stairs are steep, we can help him up."

Mahesh Jī asked, "Where is Bābūjī?" Saksenā Jī answered, "He is sitting downstairs in the garden. He is in great pain."

When privacy became available, Mahesh Jī immediately came downstairs and told us to come upstairs. Two or three people assisted in bringing me upstairs. My breathing was heavy and fast. Once upstairs, I made praṇām and sat down.

Mahārājśrī said, "Jugal Kishor! You are in great pain, aren't you? It has come as a karmic consequence. Endure it and surmount it. Guruśaran was saying to me 'may Mahārājśrī remove it,' but prārabdha karma (past actions the fruit of which are experienced now) is only removed through suffering. It can be postponed, but it cannot be eradicated completely."

I humbly said, "Mahārājśrī! I am but your child. I am under your protection. May you give me the strength needed to overcome it gladly."

Mahārājśrī looked at me with very loving eyes. I instantly felt the grace and power pervading each of my limbs.

We made our obeisance and returned home. Afterwards I had many asthma attacks, but endured them without effort through the strength given by Mahārājśrī. I kept rejoicing with every breath by doing japa with my Guru Mantra.[57] I

57 Repetition of mantras or names of a deity.

felt that I was receiving Mahārājśrī's darśan and He was saying, "Aum śāntiḥ, śāntiḥ, do not lose patience, my son."

CHAPTER 17

Success by Grace

IN the year 1961, Maharishi Mahesh Yogi organised an international conference on meditation in Rām Nagar, Rishikesh. Jagadguru Śaṅkarācārya Swami Shantananda Mahārāj (Guru Dev's successor as Śaṅkarācārya of Jyotir Maṭh) presided over it. Meditation teachers from home and abroad participated. Every day, under the guidance of Maharishi, Jagadguru Śaṅkarācārya Shantananda Mahārāj gave discourses in Hindi in the big hall. Thereafter, when some men and women eager for knowledge asked Jagadguru Mahārāj questions he gave them the proper guidance. I went there together with my family and many other friends from Jabalpur.

Maharishi Jī asked me, "Shriji, kindly translate Mahārājśrī's discourse into English. Also translate the foreigners' questions into Hindi and Mahārājśrī's answers into English."

Maharishi used the word "kindly" because he always considered me venerable, as a senior respected fellow disciple, and perhaps because I

The 1961 course in Rishikesh organized by Maharishi Mahesh Yogi and presided over by Swami Shantananda Saraswati Maharaj. Attending along with other disciples were Jugal Kishorji, his wife Kalawati Devi Ji, Umesh Ji, Brijesh Ji, daughter Rajeshwari, Janardan Prasad Upadhyaya, Ram Kishor Shrivastava, Shyam Kishor Shrivastava and Goverdhandas Shrivastava.

Jugal and Maharishi walking together at the 1961 course in Rishikesh. Jugal is on the far right, Maharishi is at center and Jugal's son Umesh is on the far left. Goverdhandas Shrivastava Jugal's cousin is second from right and Jageshwar Prasad Shrivastava (Maharishi's elder brother) second from left. Photo taken by Jugal's younger son, Brijesh Kumar Shrivastava.

was competent and blessed by the special grace of Guru Dev. Maharishi's elder brother, Shri Jāgeśvar Prasād Shrivastava, came from Jabalpur for this international meditation conference, along with Śrī J.N. Mehrā and Śrī Janārdan Prasād Upādhyāy.

I thought the task of translating would be very difficult, but Maharishi ordered it by the grace of Śrī Guru Dev. When a task is entrusted to me, then I have to do it. Each day I translated the discourses and questions accurately and faithfully.

One day some meditation teachers who had come from abroad came to my camp and began to express their gratitude. I said, "God is dwelling in everybody's heart. Our Guru Dev can also see into your hearts with eyes of compassion. He is present before everyone. Essentially there is no distinction between God and Guru Dev. They are one. Out of ignorance we consider them as separate and are therefore stuck in duality. Only by Śrī Guru's grace do such opportunities occur. By His grace alone all tasks are successfully accomplished."

CHAPTER 18

Do Japa at Any Time

AFTER my initiation in 1942, I would praise Bhagvān Śrī Guru Dev's greatness, His divinity, His capability to give welfare for all and His power and grace without cause. I would say these praises when I was with my acquaintances, relatives and other followers. I would also answer their enquiries regarding Bhagavatpūjyapād.[58]

This is true satsaṅg (discussion among aspirants about divine topics), whose purpose is to inspire one to experience for oneself the grace of a saint or of Bhagvān in a living form. It also is the cause of welfare for those possessed by māyā, giving them real grace and guidance when they are entangled in restless distress.

> "On whom God wants to show His grace, He grants the good opportunity to come under the shelter of a realised saint and who is versed in the śruti."

The vicissitudes of my life in search of a spiritual guru finally came to an end at the

58 "Holy venerable feet," an honorific title of Guru Dev.

Bhagavatpūjyapād, making me remember the scriptural verse:

> "On having found refuge, he then takes initiation from him, gets his guidance, enjoys fulfillment and reaches the accomplishment of life by getting the darśan of Bhagvān and realising the ultimate truth."

In keeping with this, I let my wife obtain initiation. Once, after initiation, we went for Guru Dev's darśan. I said to her, "If you want to ask Mahārājśrī anything, then ask him."

After we had received Guru Dev's holy darśan we were delighted. Right then my wife stood up and with folded hands asked for guidance, saying, "Mahārājśrī! All day long I am occupied with my various household chores. Sometimes I am not able to sit and do the japa meditation of the guru mantra. Therefore I feel very distressed."

It is a sign of good fortune to hear Mahārājśrī's nectar-like speech. He replied, "If you cannot do the japa meditation of the guru mantra while sitting, this is no problem. Make it your habit to do the japa of the guru mantra while standing or sitting or walking around. This is called ajapājapa. Doing this exercise again and again, it begins to become automatic. Do not allow others to hear you, otherwise they will blame you for the habit of mumbling."

My wife then asked, "Mahārājśrī! In the morning after getting up without being bathed, or being in a state of sickness, can I still do japa? And coming from the toilet, etc., in an impure condition, can I even then do the japa of the guru mantra?"

Śrī Guru Dev answered,

"Accustom yourself to do japa at every moment, that's all. In brahma muhurta,[59] in coming from the toilet, in sickness, in the cold, in the hot and the rainy season. Even when the mind does not feel like taking a bath, then begin to do japa wearing washed clothes. Japa of the guru mantra can be done under all conditions."

---

59 "Time of Brahma:" the period (muhūrta) beginning one hour and 36 minutes before sunrise and lasting 48 minutes.

CHAPTER 19

The Omniscience and Omnipotence of Guru Dev

MY Guru Dev is omniscient and omnipotent at all times. He is continually present, and for Him the limitations of the physical body do not exist. I have experienced this many times.

Paṇḍit Śrī Kuber Datta Ojhā had been going to Śrī Guru Dev for the past several years, even before 1941. When Guru Dev lived in Baldev Bāg, or during his residence in Jabalpur, Śrī Ojhā Jī provided close service to Mahārājśrī.

Out of curiosity, I often used to ask Ojhā Jī to speak of Mahārājśrī's time of sādhana. I would say, "Paṇḍit Jī! Before Mahārājśrī was appointed as Śaṅkarācārya, when He used to live in dense forests, will you not tell me something about that time, so that my belief that Mahārājśrī is trikālajña and omnipotence may be steadfast."

Ojhā Jī used to say, "No, no, Brother! Mahārājśrī has clearly ordered all residents of the āśram, brahmacharis and sanyāsīs, that if someone enquires about His early lifetime we are to refuse.

Babu Sahib! If I tell you something, then tonight Mahārājśrī will send me to my home tomorrow."

I said, "Guru Dev is on the third floor. If you tell me something here, how will He know? Paṇḍit Jī, please, tell it to me. You are my elder and most honoured brother."

Paṇḍit Kuber Datta Ojhā had one weakness. He wished to make the meal he received as a prasād (blessed food) in Guru Dev's āśram more delicious. If he could have lemon and papaya with his meal, what would he say? I knew of his weakness. When Mahārājśrī's auspicious arrival in Jabalpur took place, and Paṇḍit Ojhā Jī was part of the group, I went the next evening to the āśram and brought papaya and lemon in a bag. When Paṇḍit Jī refused to speak about Mahārājśrī's time of sādhanā, I said, "Paṇḍit Jī what would you say if there would be ripe papaya and lemon today in your meal?"

Paṇḍit Ojhā Jī refused at first, but then said, "Alright brother! You do not listen to me, so I will tell you some holy incidents. But you watch, tomorrow you will not find me in the āśram."

The next day, when I went to the āśram and found that Ojhā Jī was not there. I asked Brahmachari Mahesh Jī, "Mahesh, Ojhā Jī is not to be seen in the āśram today?"

Mahesh Jī said, "Last night, when the residents of the āśram approached Mahārājśrī one by one to make praṇām (obeisance), Mahārājśrī said, "Kuber Datta! You have not gone to your home for many days. Go stay there for a while and return afterwards." Then He gave me the instruction, "Mahesh! Give Kuber Datta a pair of dhoti[60] and some rupees and send him off tomorrow morning."

Mahesh said "I deputised an employee of the āśram to buy a dhoti. I opened the box and took out a sufficient sum. The employee bought a pair of dhoti in a nearby market, brought them to me, and gave me the remaining sum, which I gave together with the dhoti to the senior fellow disciple Śrī Ojhā Jī."

This event reinforced my belief that Śrī Guru Dev is omniscient and that His instructions should always be precisely followed.

60 A piece of cloth worn round the lower body, one end of which passes between the legs and is tucked in behind.

CHAPTER 20

The Magnetism of a Saint

ONCE Śrī Jagadguru Śaṅkarācārya Swami Brahmananda Saraswati Jī Mahārāj, after a stay in Jabalpur, was scheduled to arrive in Prayāg. The disciples of Prayāg planned a grand reception. They decided that fireworks should be exploded when the procession neared the āśram in order to alert Mahārājśrī's āśramites residing in Prayāg at Brahmanivās and Ālopī Bāg, and that there should be a second round of fireworks when the procession neared the āśram so that the saints, devotees, public figures and group of receptionists would be prepared.

At that time, Prayāg's Chief Superintendent of Police (CSP) under the British rule was a Muslim who was notorious for his strict behaviour and harsh discipline. He governed with a firm hand, like a dictator, and never allowed such celebrations.

Per government norms, the CSP's permission was necessary for such processions. It seemed highly unlikely that permission would be granted. Nonetheless, the group of welcomers submitted an application. The CSP took the application and, after reviewing it carefully, said "That will be all right." This was completely astonishing.

On the day of the procession, the CSP reached Prayāg station with a police force. When the procession set off, he saw Mahārājśrī from afar. Impressed, he showed his courtesy by slightly bowing his head. Seated on his horse, he then led the police force to the head of the procession to ensure its security.

The fireworks were set off at the beginning of the procession and again as the procession reached the āśram. The CSP neither objected nor stopped the procession. Mahārājśrī was welcomed at the āśram.

The CSP then entered the āśram. He removed his shoes, washed his hands and feet and, with permission, arrived at the door of the room where Mahārājśrī was seated. There he removed his turban, bowed to Mahārājśrī and departed in silence.

Seeing the amazing influence of Mahārājśrī's glorious stature with their own eyes, all disciples were carried away with emotion.

CHAPTER 21

The Muslim Youth

MAHĀRĀJŚRĪ was residing in the Brahmanivās āśram. He gave daily discourses that were attended by large numbers of people from different localities. Among them were Muslims, Christians, Buddhists and Jains, as well as many foreign people who came to attend the Kumbh Melā in Prayāg.

Although the foreigners did not know Hindi and could not understand the discourses, they were drawn by the magnetic attraction of the highly venerated saint. The sun shines indiscriminately on Indians, foreigners, children, youth, aged and sannyāsīs.

One day a youth came to the āśram. One of the disciples, Śrī Satyanand Gauṛ Jī, was on guard duty at the door of Mahārājśrī's room. The youth came forward and said, "Dear brother! I long to have the sight of the murśid[61] of the world. If He consents, then by seeing Him I will become happy. Please help me."

Śrī Satyanand Jī was puzzled and uncertain

61 Muslim term for a highly revered saint.

what to do. He considered inwardly the arguments pro and con. Brahmins, kṣatriyas, vaiśyas, paṇḍits, scholars, sannyāsīs and disciples used to get permission have Mahārājśrī's darśan. How could this youth, who believed in the Muslim religion, get permission?

When Satyanand Jī initially refused, the youth became carried away with emotion. His tears began to fall. He said, "Sir, I had a murśid (spiritual teacher) as my master, but he passed away many years ago. I do not know the way to worship Khuda (Muslim word for God) and therefore I have come."

Śrī Satyanand Gaur, who was later known as Śrī Swami Satyanand, and who accompanied Maharishi Mahesh Yogi to propagate transcendental meditation for many years, was at a loss how to respond. Seeking guidance, he went to Mahārājśrī and explained everything. After some silence, Mahārājśrī said, "Send him here."

When Satyanand Gauṛ Jī went downstairs and informed this youth that permission had been granted, the youth was greatly delighted and went into Mahārājśrī's room. When he returned after about half an hour, an amazing peace glowed over his face and his eyes were filled with tears. He said, "Sir, I cannot forget your favour. I am deeply convinced that he is the most perfect murśid in the whole world. He told me the path ahead and

I have become happy. Henceforth he is my kamil murśid (learned master)." After saying this he embraced me.

CHAPTER 22

Faith in the Guru's Capacity

ON the banks of the holy river Yamuna in Delhi, for the sake of the worshipping of Bhagvān Śaṅkar's (Shiva's) great goddess, the "Śatmukh Koṭi Homātmak" mahāyajña (great sacrifice) had been organised under the patronage of Mahārājśrī. Numerous disciples from different regions and towns had arrived. Camps were set up at the sand-bank of the Yamuna for their stay. Our group of fellow disciples from Jabalpur stayed together with their families in tents near the yajña (sacrifice) to hear the upadeś (spiritual instructions).

I volunteered in the service of Mahārājśrī's camp. When I got two tents, I brought my family from my cousin Śrī Sādhurām Shrivastava's railway quarters in Mathurā. My family and other fellow disciples stayed in these two tents for the sake of the parikramā (circumambulation) of the yajñaśālā[62] and for hearing Mahārājśrī's discourses.

Every morning volunteers came to the tents to

62 Hall of sacrifice: place for keeping the sacrificial fire; temple.

give the families milk and laḍḍūs.[63] At noon meals of prasād were distributed free of charge to everyone at the restaurant near to the yajña-maṇḍap.[64] According to the Mahārājśrī's order, all were to be fed until their family says, "We have received enough, please do not give more."

Yet some fellow disciples would continue taking more, even when their wives tried to stop them. These fellow disciples, in their greed, asked for more as a snack and put them in bags.

Upon seeing their greed, I felt pity for them, because everything of this kind would be served again in the evening. Where did they keep the laḍḍūs? They made a kind of pit in the sand and squeezed them, bound in cloth, into the sand. How strange was the greed of those hard-hearted people, who had no faith in the strength of the sadguru. We must say of such people:

> "They came here clean and pure, but māyā (illusion) polluted them.
> They found refuge in the guru, but they are trapped in the shackles of doubt."

63 A traditional Indian sweet.

64 Pavilion built for the yajña.

CHAPTER 23

Riddhi and Siddhi

THE necessary supplies for the "Śatmukh Koṭi Homātmak" mahāyajña (great sacrifice) arrived from north, south, east and west by various means, such as bullock cart, truck, etc. These supplies were then stored in warehouses.

Once I asked a driver of a bullock cart, "Brother, from where are you coming?" Pointing towards the north he said, "From the northern side of Delhi." I then said, "Sacks of sugar are in your bullock cart, well, who has sent you?" He said, "I do not know the name, but he paid me full cartage in advance."

I asked the same questions to the others driving trucks and tractors. They would name the place from where they came, and also say that they did not know the sender, but the cartage was paid in full and they were not to seek further payment at the destination site. All efforts to learn the identity of sender were in vain.

This reminded me of the reception at the āśram of Saint Bharadvāj in Prayāg at this very location as narrated in the Rāmcaritmānas of Gosvāmī

Tulsīdās. Bharat, the younger brother of Śrī Rām, arrived together with Sadguru Śrī Vaśiṣṭha Jī and other sanyāsīs, father Śrī Darśarath Jī's three queens, respectively mothers, townspeople and army personnel in great numbers. Then Bharat Jī arrived and paid a visit to the saint Bharadvāj. The trikālajña Mahātmā Śrī Bharadvāj understood that Bharat Jī was not alone and that a large number of residents of Ayodhyā had come with him. Seeing Bharat's affection towards his eldest brother Śrī Rām, Muni Śrī Bharadvāj said,

> "Oh Tāt[65]! Do not grieve too much; by having darśan of the feet of Śrī Rāmcandra alone, all sorrow is eliminated. Become our valued guest. Please take your night's rest here and accept vegetable, roots, fruits and flowers and whatever we may offer." He said to his disciples, "We have to be hospitable to Bharat."

The disciples said, "Oh Master! Very good!" After saying this they bowed their heads and each departed in the direction of their work.

The Saint became worried. The guests were highly honoured and had to be entertained on par with their greatness. Seeing the saint's concern, the deities of affluence, Riddhi and Siddhi, arrived.

65 Affectionate term of address, esp. to a junior person.

Riddhi and Siddhi asked the saint, "Please tell us what needs to be done."

The saint became delighted and said, "Bharat Jī and the younger brother Śatrughan in his company suffer the anguish of separation from Śrī Rām. Arrange for their reception and make them fresh for the rest of the journey."

Riddhi and Siddhi immediately created beautiful mansions, each having affluent luxury items, excellent food, drinks of all varieties and many unimaginable things that would make even demigods desirous of them. Each mansion was staffed with male and female servants who were alert and dutiful and prepared to offer everything that was required. Śrī Bharadvāj Muni then gave permission for Bharat Jī and his family to stay.

A similar situation happened in Mahārājśrī's camp, too. One might suppose Riddhis and Siddhis were ready to serve, and nobody had any kind of shortage. The trikālajña, omnipotent Jagadguru Śaṅkarācārya Mahārājśrī, bringer of the welfare of the world, graced this noble land to guide mankind on the path of virtue. This is my firm conviction.

CHAPTER 24

Divine Aid

ŚRĪ Rāj Rājeśvarī Prasād Varmā was the paternal uncle of fellow-disciple Śrī Jāgeśvar Prasād Shrivāstav Jī. He owned a photography studio called C.P. Photo Art Studio at Maṛhātāl in Jabalpur. Śrī Varmā Jī lived together with his family in Jabalpur at Andheradev on the first floor. Among Guru Dev's disciples in Jabalpur, he was the most senior. He has written a book in English about Guru Dev and was the paternal uncle of Brahmachari Mahesh Jī.

In 1948, Śrī Rāj Rājeśvarī Prasād Varmā planned for a child. For some unknown reason, the 7-8 month old offspring twisted in the womb of his wife, Śrīmatī Varmā, and died prematurely. The body of the infant was blue. This deeply affected Śrīmatī Varmā, and all the dependents also became distressed. They pinned their hopes on Guru Dev Jagadguru Śaṅkarācārya Mahārājśrī, thinking only He could do something, and they contemplated on Him.

Śrī Guru Dev directed paṇḍit Dvārkā Prasād

Śāstrī Jī to draw a yantra (secret diagram) on a piece of paper and said,

> "Wash it with milk, pour its fluid into a bowl and tell Brahmachari Mahesh Jī that he has to immediately take the bowl filled with the fluid to Śrī Rāj Rājeśvarī Prasād Varmā."

In those days, Mahārājśrī's residence was in the koṭhī (large house, bungalow) of the prosperous merchant Rādhākṛṣṇa in Gañjīpura, Jabalpur, which was at a distance of around 200-300 yards. He ordered that the consecrated water in this bowl should be kept carefully, without being spilled.

Śrīcaraṇ's instructions were carried out and Mahesh Jī departed. About 10-15 minutes later, he arrived at Śri Varmā's house. As he climbed the stairs he encountered Śrī Varmā Jī coming down. He said, "Mahesh! Your aunt is protected, but a dead child, who has turned completely blue, has been removed from her womb. Your auntie's body was also turning blue."

Śrī Mahesh said, "Uncle! According to the directions of Mahārājśrī, let aunt drink the consecrated water in this bowl, then she will quickly regain complete health."

This was done immediately. The next day Śri Varmā went together with his wife to Mahārājśrī to bow at his lotus feet. Many such incidents occurred suddenly from time to time, whereby our faith and devotion at the feet of Guru Dev kept growing.

CHAPTER 25

The Most Fortunate in the World

THOSE devotees and disciples of Guru Dev who followed the instructions given by Mahārājśrī on the day of their initiation, by which the antaḥkarṇa[66] gradually kept becoming pure, began to experience the grace of the guru. Not only this, they experienced the effect of Guru Dev's divine powers, became knowledgeable in regard of their iṣṭa[67] deva and abounded in bhakti without any other desires, because:

> "Those who love their guru's lotus feet,
> they are considered fortunate in the world
> and in the Veda."[68]

Among such very fortunate ones was Śrī Shantanand Saraswati. He was assigned the seat of Jagadguru Śaṅkarācārya according to Śrī Guru Dev's last will. Brahmachari Mahesh, who later

66 The most inner being.

67 Chosen god or goddess.

68 Passage from Śrī Rāmcaritmānas.

became famous as Maharishi Mahesh Yogi, and some other devotees too, these fortunate persons always reflect the divinity received from Guru Dev and are engaged full time in activities of Lok-Kalyan (benefiting the world).

In the year 1963, when I received news that my eldest son, Ch. Umesh Kumar Shrivastava, was appointed a lecturer in Durga College in Raipur, I approached my senior and most excellent fellow-disciple Śrī Śhantanand Saraswati Mahārājśrī in Miśrabandhu Kāryālay Dīkṣitpurā, Jabalpur, to request his permission to send my eldest son to Raipur. When I made this request, Mahārājśrī remained quiet for a minute and then said, "All right, send him."

One of my sons was appointed in Raipur, the other to Bhopal, and I had been retired since 1957. Hence, I have lived with my wife and my daughter Ku. Rājeśvarī at my residence at 954, in Bāī kā Bagīcā, Jabalpur. My heartfelt wish was that one son would stay with me, but for the sake of my children's future, I carried out Mahārājśrī's order immediately.

After this, by the efforts of one of my fellow-disciples, Śrī Mānikalāl Mālpāṇī Jī, I tried to get employment for my son at the Govindrām Seksāriyā Commerce College in Jabalpur. Just when this seemed quite possible, suddenly the appointment was deferred. Subsequently, even after making several efforts, my eldest son could not be appointed to Jabalpur. The directive of Śaṅkarācārya Mahārājśrī seated on Mahārājśrī's position remained impervious and unchanging.

According to Śrī Guru Dev's instructions, and in line with the request by Dr. Kogar and Dr. Śilp made at the international philosophical conference held in Calcutta in 1950, Śrī Brahmachari Mahesh Jī adopted the boon of the simple method of deep meditation for the sake of the welfare of the world, and started to come out to distribute the blessing of transcendental meditation, bringing about the well-being of seekers in many countries who desire for their own good fortune.

Those very fortunate sevaks[69] of the feet of Guru Dev always revere their guru. They are very fortunate, natural, simple and wise, and always engaged in the service of others.

69 A servant, worshipper, disciple.

—JAI ŚRĪ GURU DEV—

APPENDIX

1.

A Tribute to the Shrivastava Family

IT was the connection with Swami Brahmananda Saraswati, the former Śaṅkarācārya of Jyotir Maṭh, that united the Guru Dev Legacy Trust and the Shrivastava family. The main family seat today is still located in Raipur, Chhattisgarh, India.

Over three generations this family has incorporated and passed down a strong personal and devotional link with Guru Dev and his teachings. The family has amassed and preserved a unique treasury of those teachings. These include Hindi transcripts of many previously unpublished discourses of Guru Dev, as well as correspondence with Guru Dev and with Maharishi Mahesh Yogi.

We are very fortunate that the current family members are carrying on this heritage and wholeheartedly supporting the Trust in spreading the teachings of Guru Dev.

JUGAL KISHOR SHRIVASTAVA (1902–1970)

The author of these reminiscences was born in 1902 in the village of Khurai in the Sagar District of Madhya Pradesh, India. His parents were Laxman Prasad Shrivastava (1870-1940) and Kuwar Devi Shrivastava (1878-1958). Both were deeply spiritual. Jugal said that his mother "always lived in the lap of God." His father, Jugal said, "inculcated in me the fervour of spirituality, motivated me to write literature, taught me to be resolute in the face of the vicissitudes of worldly life and inspired me with the divine glory of Rāmcaritmānas, which he could recite from memory."

Following his education, he became an officer in the engineering department of the Great Indian Peninsula Railway in Jabalpur, India. Highly skilled in all aspects of railway planning, he was loved and respected by his seniors and juniors alike.

Jugal lived in Jabalpur with his wife, Smt. Kalavati Shrivastava, and their four children, consisting of two sons and two daughters, with the elder son being Umesh. Throughout his life, Jugal had a deep interest in religion, philosophy, and the quest for spiritual enlightenment. He loved to read the epic Rāmāyaṇa and was eventually able to recite it from memory. He was well versed in Sanskrit, Hindi and English language and literature and, during his young age, wrote poems and articles published in renowned magazines like "Saraswati."

In 1942, when he was 40 years of age, Jugal saw Guru Dev riding on an elephant in a religious procession in Jabalpur and knew instantly that he had found the teacher he had sought for so long. Soon thereafter he and his wife took spiritual initiation from the Guru Dev.

Jugal was blessed to have very close contact with Guru Dev for many years, experiencing time and again his most generous, empathetic, pioneering and all-embracing personality. Fortunately, Jugal took care to write down his recollections of Guru Dev. By the end of his life, Jugal found that deep peace and joy that comes from spiritual awakening. He passed away at the age 68 in 1970, seated comfortably with eyes closed with his mind absorbed in his beloved Lord Rāma.

After Guru Dev departed Jabalpur at the end of chaturmas each year, he often directed many disciples to contact Jugal Kishor for resolution of their minor mundane problems, as Guru Dev observed the divine potential of Jugal and graced him with the capability of rendering service to others.

Photograph taken on February 12, 1961, in the puja room of Shri Jugal Kishor Shrivastavaji's house at Baī Kā Bagīcā in Jabalpur. Jugal is standing at the right. Seated at the right is Swami Vishnudevananda Saraswati ji Maharaj, who succeeded Swami Shantanand Maharaj as the Shankaracharya of Jyotir Maṭh. The guru brothers standing on the left are Janardan Prasad Upadhyay, Shri Ramesh Ji (who made the wooden temple of Guru Dev in this photo) and Chandrashekhar Sahay Saxena Ji.

UMESH SHRIVASTAVA (1940–2021)

Umesh was born on Sunday, September 4, 1940, in the cultured city of Jabalpur, India. In 1966, Umeshjī married Smt. Kiran Shrivastava, who was also a person with a deep spiritual inclination.

Beginning in 1963, Umesh served as the

professor of commerce and, in the later years, as head of the department of Business Management, at the prestigious Durga Mahavidyalaya of Raipur, Chhattisgarh, serving there for a marathon span of 34 years. From his early years he had keen interest in Hindi literature. He used to participate in debate competitions and in Gita and Ramayana recitations.In addition, he wrote articles in various magazines, including "Kalyan," published by the Gita press in Gorakhpur, India.

Umesh lived his life in accord with the teachings of Pūjanīya Śrī Guru Dev and never gave greater importance to the materialistic accolades. His pure and exemplary lifestyle and profound devotion at the lotus feet of Pūjanīya Guru Dev and Lord Rāma fostered a strong bonding and deep affection among his three sons.

Within the framework of the pious teachings of Poojaya Guru Dev, Umesh always awoke at four in the morning, practicing meditation, ajapājapa (spontaneous continuous silent chanting) and listening to bhajans. His entire life was altruistically dedicated to the conservation, preservation and encouragement of the legacy of Pūjanīya Śrī Guru Dev. He was a staunch follower and promoter of the simple system of deep meditation originally devised by Poojya Śrī Guru Dev and spread throughout the world by Maharishi Mahesh Yogi.

With his daily practice of meditation and the study of scriptures, Umesh was the perfect role model of a true disciple of Guru Dev. He was filled with peace and joy and dedicated his life to spreading that peace and joy to everyone he encountered.

Umesh established the Swami Brahmananda Saraswati Seva Sansthan in the year 2007 at Raipur to promote the teachings of Pūjanīya Śrī Guru Dev and the Rāmcaritmānas for the benefit of all succeeding generations. This organisation published many important books, including "Vedanta Incarnate: My Master," written in Hindi by Maharishi Mahesh Yogi and translated to English by Jugal Kishor Shrivastava. Umesh also carefully preserved the manuscript of the reminiscences of his beloved father and resolved to have them published in English for the benefit of people everywhere.

Maharshi Mahesh Yogi shared emotional bonding both with Jugal and Umeshjī beginning from their early days together in Jabalpur, India. Maharshi maintained this connection even from the headquarters of his movement, first in Switzerland and later in the Netherlands.

Shri Umeshjī was a highly esteemed board member of the Trust. He inspired and guided the Trust with his unbounded kindness and love. The Trust was deeply moved by his unexpected passing away on December 4, 2021, and by the passing a year later of his beloved wife, Smt. Kiran Shrivastava. Inspired by Umesh, the Trust remains committed to fulfilling his wish that the divine wisdom of Guru Dev reach people everywhere.

BRIJESH KUMAR SHRIVASTAVA (1942)

Shri Brijesh Kumar Shrivastava is the younger brother of Shri Umesh Kumar Shrivastava. They were both blessed to be the sons of Shri Jugal Kishor Shrivastava, a great scholar of Hindi, Sanskrit, and English literature and a devoted follower of Swami Brahmananda Saraswati, the Shankaracharya of Jyotir Maṭh.

Maharishi Mahesh Yogi visited Jabalpur in early 1961 and personally initiated both brothers and their younger sister into transcendental meditation. Shri Jugal Kishor Shrivastava was the chairman of the reception committee that welcomed Maharishi to Jabalpur and he, along with both brothers and other Gurubhāīs, actively participated in the welcome activities and in organizing Maharishi's lectures to the intellectual community of Jabalpur.

Brijesh's wife was also subsequently initiated into transcendental mediation by Shri Jugal Kishor Shrivastavaji. Brijesh believes that all family members, including his brothers and sisters, have led successful lives due to the spiritual teachings of

Bhagwan Gurudeva, under the guidance of their beloved father. None of their family members experienced premature death or any adverse incidents. Instead, they have always been shielded from calamities. In the worldly affairs, they have prospered, all due to the blessings of His Divinity.

As Maharaj Shri often said, it is not right to interfere with the results of past karmas endured in this life. But as Brijesh said, the grace of His Divinity greatly fortifies the inner self of a devotee such that their suffering is greatly alleviated.

SANJAY SHRIVASTAVA (1967)

As the eldest of the three sons of Umeshjī, Sanjay, together with his brothers Amit and Manish, is continuing the family's steadfast devotion to Guru Dev as a highly honourable board member of the Guru Dev Legacy Trust. The entire collection of original literature, including Guru Dev's teaching and other artifacts, is now being carefully preserved in his safekeeping. He is committed to continuing his family's tradition of maintaining, preserving and publishing all the original materials related to Poojya Shri Guru Dev preserved by his grandfather Jugal Kishor Shrivastava and his father Umesh Kumar Shrivastava. He is most humbly dedicated to this work as his life's mission.

2.1

A Letter Dictated by Swami Brahmananda Saraswati to Jugal Kishor Shrivastava

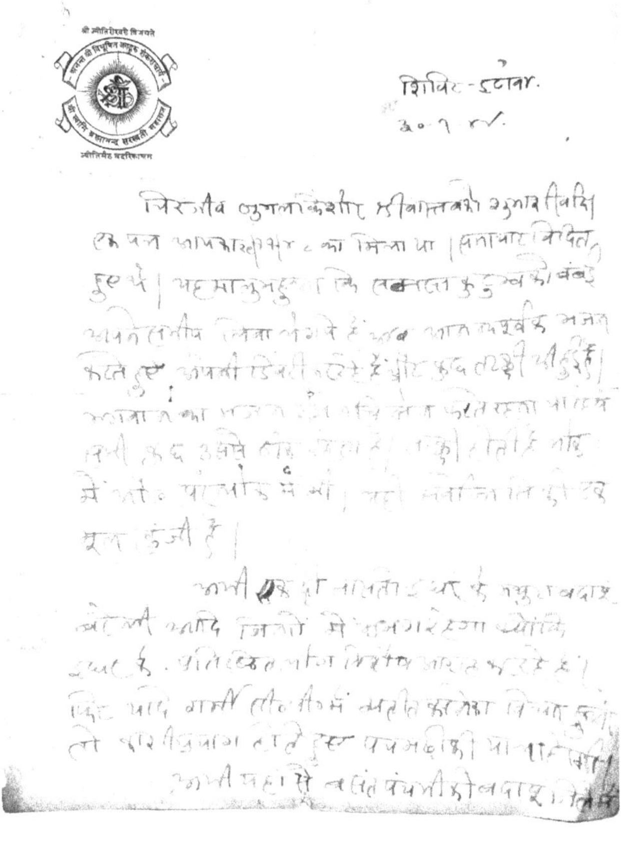
श्री ज्योतिरीश्वरो विजयते

ज्योतिर्मठ बदरिकाश्रम

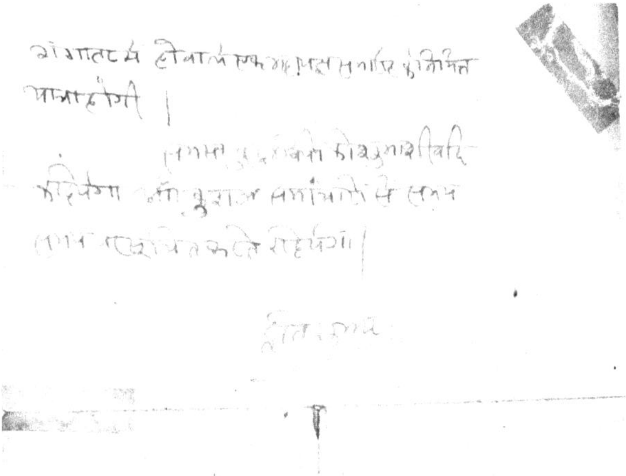

शिविर- इटावा
30-01-49

चिरंजीव जुगलकिशोर श्रीवास्तव को शुभाशिर्वाद ।

एक पत्र आपका 29/11/48 का मिला था। समाचार विदित हुए थे। यह मालुम हुआ कि समस्त कुटुम्ब को बंबई अपने समीप लिवा ले गये है, अब आनन्दपूर्वक भजन करते हुए अपनी डिवटी कर रहे है और कुछ तरक्की भी हुई है। भगवान का भजन पूजन चिन्तन करते रहना चाहिये। सभी कुछ उससे ठीक रहता है। तरक्की होती है, लोक परलोक में भी। यही सर्वोन्नतिकी एक मूल कुंजी है।

अभी कुछ मास तो इधर के मथुरा बदायूं बरेली आदि जिलों में भ्रमण रहेगा क्योंकि इधर के प्रतिष्ठित लोग विशेष आग्रह कर रहे है। फिर यदि गर्मी सी.जी. में व्यतीत करने का विचार हुआ तो काशीप्रयाग होते हुए पचमढ़ी की यात्रा होगी।

अभी यहां से बसंत पंचमी को बदायूं जिले में गंगातर में सेवाये एक महायज्ञ समारोह के निमित्त यात्रा होगी।

समस्त कुटुम्बियों को शुभाशीर्वाद कहियेगा और कुशल समाचारों से समय समय पर सूचित करते रहियेगा।

इतिशुभम्

CAMP – ITAWA
30.01.1949

With good blessings to Chiranjeev Shri Jugalkishor Ji Shrivastava.

A letter dated 29.11.1948 was received from you. I was apprised of the news .It was learnt through your letter that , you have taken your family along with you to Bambai (Bombay) and now are performing your duty pleasantly, simultaneously continuing the lord's worship and also have been promoted recently. It is a must to perform Lord's bhajan poojan (chanting GOD's name, meditating and worshiping GOD) for every individual, which ushers into all good happenings. One gets promoted in this materialistic world (Loka) as well as in the world beyond this materialistic world (Paraloka). This is the sole prime key for all round prosperity.

For the next one or two months , the visit to the nearby districts of Mathura, Badayun and Bareli is scheduled due to the persistent special requests of the elite citizens of these areas. Later; if desired; to spend the summer season in the C.P. , then the journey to the Panchamadhri would be performed through Kashi, Prayaga.

From here, on the auspious day of Basant Panchami, the journey to the Badayun distric would be performed where a grand Yagya is scheduled on the banks of the river Ganges.

Convey my good blessings to all the members of your family and continue apprising me of the news of the wellness at your end.

(Eti Shubham) It is enough for the moment with wishes for all the well in future

2.2

A Letter from Maharishi Mahesh Yogi to Jugal Kishor Shrivastava

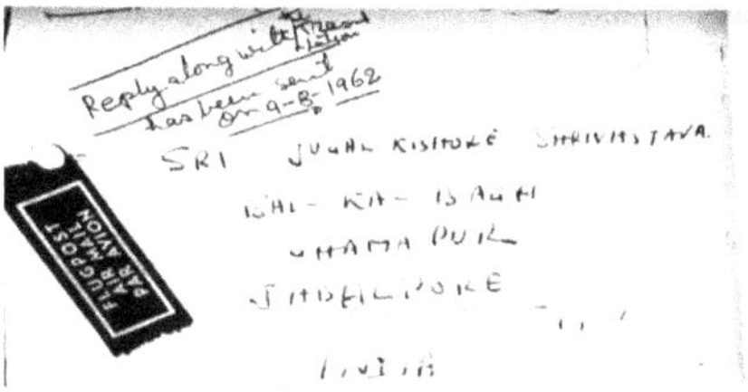

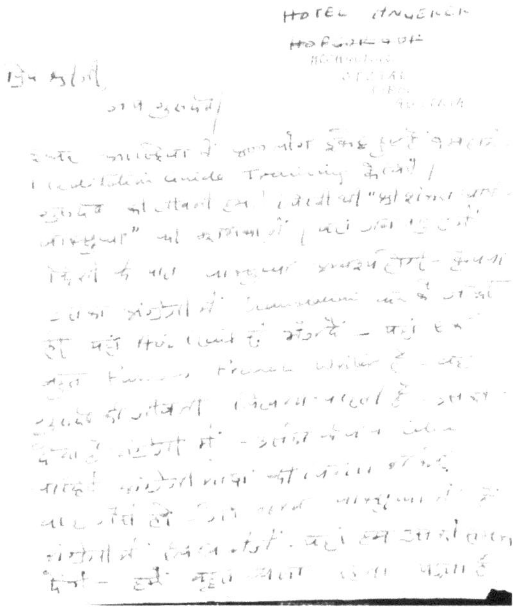

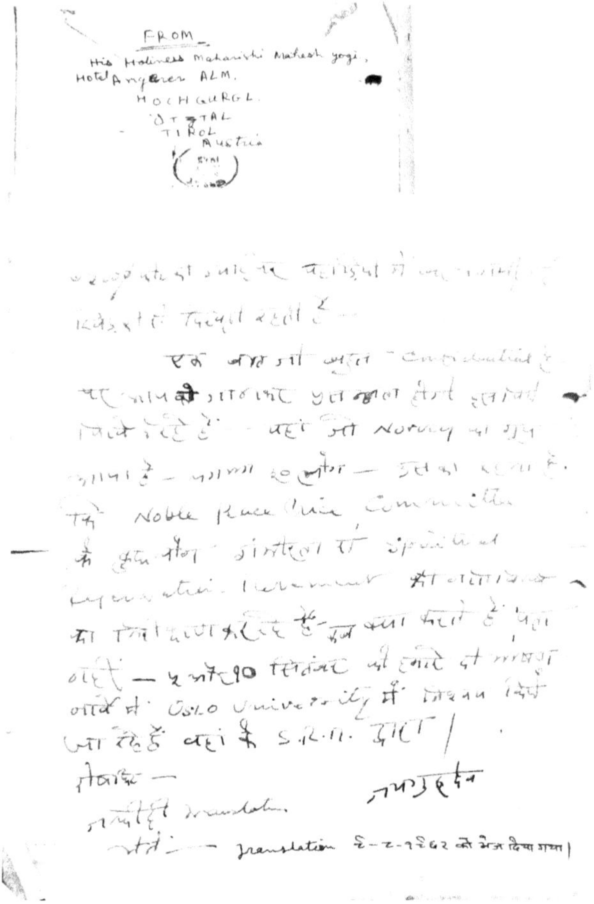

FROM
His Holiness Maharishi Mahesh yogi,
Hotel Angerer ALM.
HOCHGURGL
ÖTZTAL
TIROL
Austria

[illegible]

एक बात और बहुत Congratulation [illegible]
[illegible]
[illegible] यहां [illegible] Norway [illegible]
[illegible]
[illegible] Noble Peace Prize Committee
के [illegible] spiritual
regeneration movement [illegible]
[illegible]
[illegible] — ५ और १० सितम्बर [illegible]
[illegible] Oslo University में [illegible]
जा रहे हैं वहां के S.R.M. द्वारा।
[illegible] —
[illegible] translation
[illegible] — Translation ६-८-१९६२ को भेज दिया गया।

HOCHGURGL
OTZTAL
TIROL
AUSTRIA

Dear Shriji,

Jai Gurudeva,

Here in Austria around 400 people have gathered in one month for the Meditation Guide Training. I have written the biography of Gurudeva in form of "Shankaracharya Vaak-Sudha". There in Jabalpur certainly someone must have the copy of Vaaksudha. – Kindly translate the same in English and arrange to send the same at the earliest here via-Airmail. Here is a very famous French writer, who desires to write the biography of Gurudeva, the English translation of Vaak Sudha has to be handed over to her. She needs only the idea, kindly do not worry about the English language, in whatever way, the feeling expressed in Vaaksudha needs to be translated in English, I will explain here in Austria. I am extremely busy these days.

The snow cladded mountain at the altitude of 7500 feet is visible from the window of my room.

I would like to share a very confidential information, though being confidential since it would please you, so I am writing to you: "Here the visiting group from Norway – approximately 30 people – have been saying that the some members of the Nobel Peace Prize Committee are seriously observing the activities of the Spiritual Regeneration Movement- what actions will be initiated and when, this is not known" .

My two lectures are being scheduled by the S.R.M movement, there in the Oslo University on September 5 and 10 .

Rest Later,
Jai Gurudeva,

N.B. – Kindly send the translation at the earliest.

Translation sent on 9.8.1962.

Note:

Maharishi never wrote Jugal Kishore ji`s name because he offers him so much respect that he always used "Shri" as prefix and "Ji" as suffix to give and honor him as per Indian tradition.

2.3

A Second Letter from Maharishi Mahesh Yogi to Jugal Kishor Shrivastava

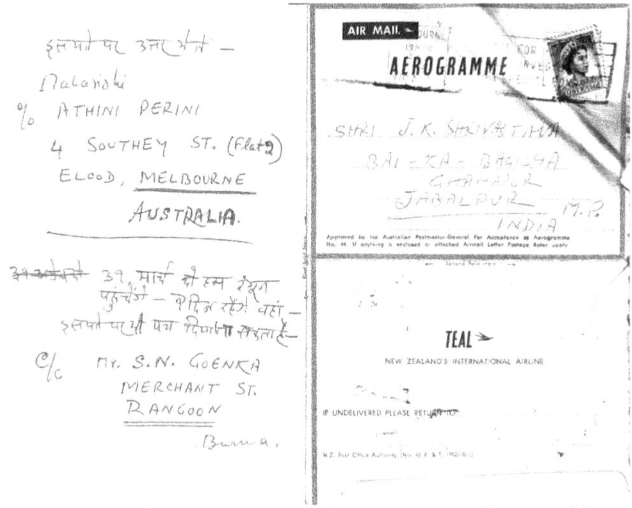
इस पते पर उत्तर भेजें —
Maharishi
℅ ATHINI PERINI
4 SOUTHEY ST. (Flat 2)
ELOOD, MELBOURNE
AUSTRALIA.

31 मार्च को हम रंगून पहुंचेंगे — कुछ दिन रहेंगे वहां —
इस पते पर भी पत्र दिया जा सकता है —
C/o Mr. S.N. GOENKA
MERCHANT ST.
RANGOON
Burma.

AIR MAIL
AEROGRAMME
SHRI J. K. SHRIVASTAVA
BAI-KA-BAGICHA
GHAMAPUR
JABALPUR M.P.
INDIA
Approved by the Australian Postmaster-General for Acceptance as Aerogramme No. 44. If anything is enclosed or attached Airmail Letter Postage Rates apply
TEAL
NEW ZEALAND'S INTERNATIONAL AIRLINE
IF UNDELIVERED PLEASE RETURN TO:

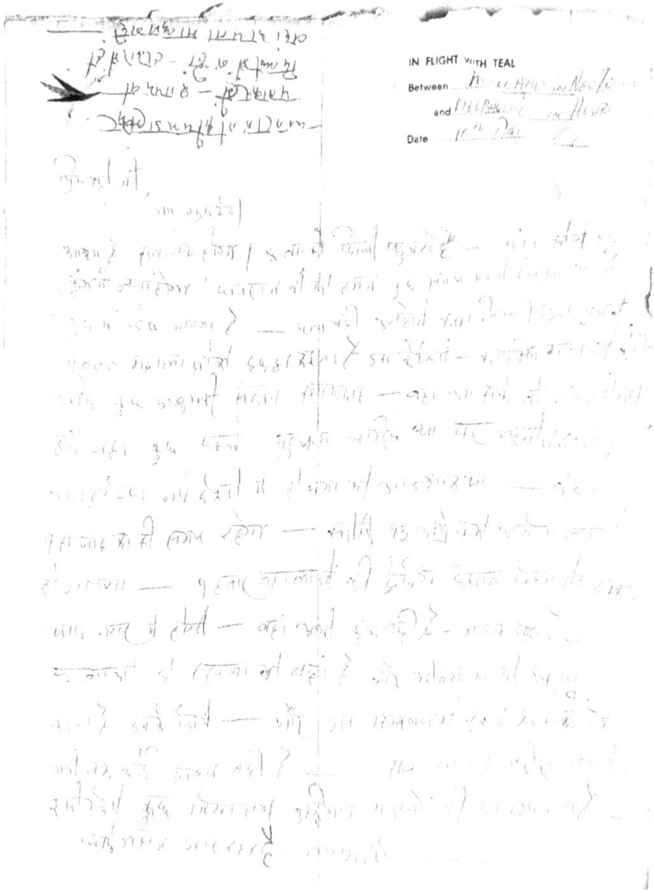
IN FLIGHT WITH TEAL
Between
and
Date

Date 16 March 62.

Dear SRI JI,

Jai Gurudeva,

It is hoped that everything is fine. Reaching Delhi on 4 th of April. From there directly will proceed to Haridwar for Kumbh. I had written to Dhanrajji some time back that a camping has to be done there in Kumbh, it is not known what action he has taken in this regard. We have to gather 1000 gentlemen (Mahatmas) during this Kumbh. To handle the responsibility in this regard, it would be good if some experience and knowledgeable gentlemen could reach there at Kumbh. I should have reached there earlier but is was equally necessary to be there in these new countries viz. Australia and New Zealand- we would be left with only a week's time as the Last Holy Bath shall take place on 13 April. The training and meditation center for the 1000 gentlemen is planned at Shankaracharya Nagar - As of now there is nothing available there except the Jungle - We have to make gentlemen stay there also arrangement for the food also needs to be made. - as of now there is no arrangement for meeting the expenditure in this regard- All will have to take place as per the God's Wishes. - It is therefore, few honest and intelligent people are required- The aircraft is descending now- JAI GURUDEVA.

Note: Enquire about Dhanrajji by dropping a letter - perhaps he might not be in Delhi but in Haridwar. Address there is not known.

Send the reply at the following address:

MAHARISHI

C/O ATHINI PERINI

4, SOUTHEY ST .(Flat 2)

ELOOD - MELBOURNE

AUSTRALIA

On 31 March will reach Rangoon- Stay there for 2 days - The letter may be sent at the following address too:

C/o Mr. S.N. GOENKA

MERCHANT ST.

RANGOON, Burma

2.4

A Letter from JP Shrivastava (Maharishi's Brother) to Umesh Shrivastava

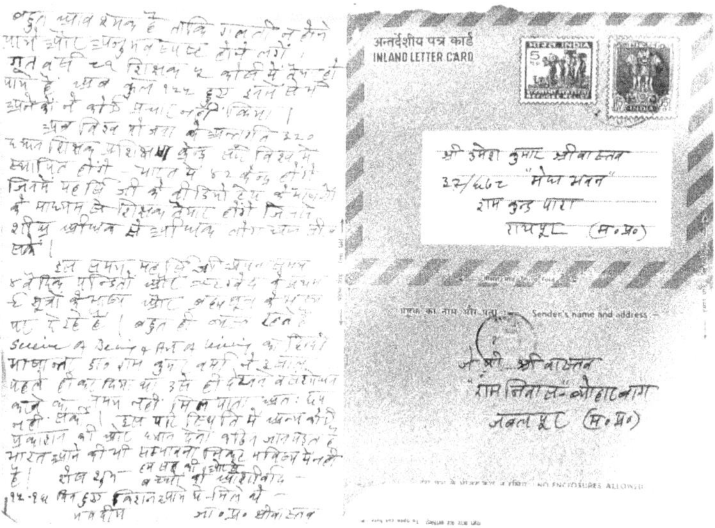

अन्तर्देशीय पत्र कार्ड
INLAND LETTER CARD

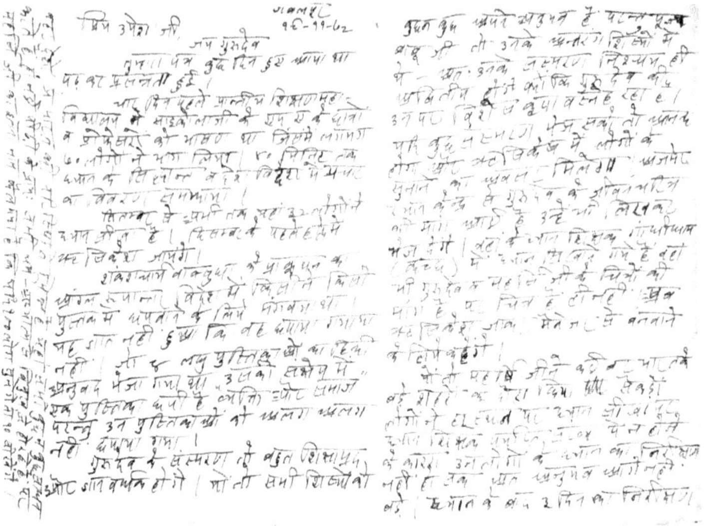
जबलपुर
१६-११-६२
प्रिय उमेश जी,
जय गुरुदेव

Jabalpur
19-11-72

Dear Shri Umeshji,

Jai Gurudeva,

Your letter had come few days ago. It brought delight to me. Four days ago, in the department of Psychology at provincial college here a speech has been delivered by me before a gathering of around 70 students and Professors wherein the principle of the meditation and its dissemination at global level has been elaborated.

Around 32 people have learnt the meditation since September. I will go to Rishikesh in the month of December. The English translation of the preface of Shankaracharya Vaak Sudha had been requisitioned by some one from abroad for publishing in some book, but it is not known whether the same has been published or not. The Hindi translation of four small booklets have been summarized and published in form of as single book entitled as "Vayakti aur Samaj", but those booklets have not been published individually.

The reminiscences of Gurudeva shall be definitely be lesson worthy and enlightening. Despite the fact that each disciple of Gurudeva has his own experience with Shri Gurudeva, but Poojaniya Babuii belonged to one among close confidants of Gurudeva, so reminisces written by Poojaniya Babuji shall be unparalleled, because he has been fortunate enough to receive special blessings and affection of Gurudeva. I will be delighted should I receive some of those reminiscences, it would give me an opportunity to share them with others in Rishikesh. The meditation center of Ajmer has solicited the Biography of Gurudeva, it will be sent to them. The mediation teachers of that center are currently visiting Gandhi Dham(Katcha) , there also exists a demand for the portraits of Gurudeva and Maharshi but they are not available with us. The manager at Rishikesh will be requested for taking action for making of the portraits.

Though Maharshi had been to several big cities of Bharat and hundreds of people have learnt the meditation during his visit but due to non-availability of mediation teachers in sufficient numbers, inspection could not be materialled post their learning the mediation. Therefore, the experiences of these people could not be collected. It is necessary to carry out inspection within three days with respect to the people who have learnt the meditation, so that no error is committed in the meditation process and the experiences become clear. Last year 81 teachers have been trained totaling the no of trained teachers to 155, but many among them have not propagated the meditation technique further. Now as per the global policy, 350 no of training centers for the meditation teachers will be established in which 42 centers will be in India, where with the aid of the video tapes of Maharshi, the teachers will be trained, in turn enabling more and more no of people to learn the mediation at the earliest. At present Mahershiji is devoting his time with the, Vaidic Scholars and the Bhashya of the First Sutras of the Rigveda and the Bhashya of Bramhasutra. He is extremely busy nowadays. The Hindi translation of the "Science of being and art of living "had been completed by Dr. Ramkumar Verma, three years before, but Maharshi could not spare time for the perusal and necessary corrections in it. Therefore, it could not be published in Hindi. At this juncture it appears difficult to pay attention to any new publication. There are no immediate possibilities for his arrival in India in near future.

The situation here in India is different than that existing abroad. Here in India, people practice spirituality in some or the other way though the, majority of the new generation is apparently distracted from the spirituality and dharma. As Marshi's name is so much popular so if 100 persons listen to him then at least 10 will definitely learn the meditation

The blessings to all the children from all of us here,

Rest is OK.

N.B. 15-16 days before, Shri Kishan had visited us,

Sender ,

J.P.Shrivastava

3.0

A Short Biography of Swami Brahmananda Saraswati (1870-1953)

SWAMI Brahmananda Saraswati was a highly revered Indian saint who, from 1941 to 1953, occupied the seat of the Śaṅkarācārya of Jyotir Maṭh, the highest position of spiritual leadership in north India. Referred to by his followers respectfully as Guru Dev (Divine Teacher), Swami Brahmananda was widely recognised to be one of those rare saints who is both expertly versed in the Vedic texts and fully spiritually realized.

As Śaṅkarācārya, Swami Brahmananda unified and harmonised the different schools of Indian philosophy and religious thought and ushered in a major spiritual revival throughout the Indian subcontinent. Universally respected, he was lauded by the first President of India as "Vedanta Incarnate," the very embodiment of Supreme Truth.

Swami Brahmananda taught that guruhood is immortal, eternal and indestructible, like electric power. We need only connect to it by pressing the button of the sādhana (spiritual practices), and thereby illuminating the light bulb in the form of the heart. In this way, we can gain complete salvation even while living in this world.

Swami Brahmananda spent most of his life in seclusion and only accepted the position of Śaṅkarācārya after years of persuasion. From that time forward he became more accessible to the public. Wherever he went vast throngs of people would gather to have his darśan and listen with rapt attention to his discourses.

Guru Dev was born in a prosperous, well-educated Brahmin family in a village near Ayodhya in Uttar Pradesh on December 21, 1870. At the age of nine, he became an ascetic, renouncing worldly life. He resolved to find a guru with the characteristics prescribed by the holy scriptures. It necessarily took time for him to find such a guru, but owing to faith and patience his aspiration was fulfilled. In the remote valley of Uttarkashi in the Himalayas he found a sage who was well versed in the Vedas and dedicated to God. This sage was Swami Krishnananda Saraswati Mahārāj. From him he received spirtitual initiation and stayed near him for twelve years until he completed his study of the scriptures and perfected his practice of yoga.

He then came down from the Himalayas and began to dwell in the uninhabited dense forests in central India. He stayed there for many years, living in caves in the solitude of thick jungles.

At the age of 36, he reunited with his guru at Prayāg during the Khumb Mela and received from him his final initiation, this time into the sannyās order. In the year 1941, on the occasion of the ninth plenary session of the general committee of the all-Indian Sanātana Dharma, Swami Brahmananda was consecrated as the Śaṅkarācārya of Jyotir Maṭh, thereby occupying a seat that had been vacant for 165 years.

Swami Brahmananda with Dr. Rajendra Prasad, the first president of India (Delhi, December 4, 1952)

During the next twelve years Swami

Brahmananda traveled widely throughout north India, presiding at religious events and giving discourses. Wherever he spoke, people spontaneously felt their doubts removed and problems solved. He also organised holy sacrifices in Delhi, Mumbai and Benares, and properly administered the monastery of Jyotir Maṭh. On the 20th May 1953, Swami Brahmananda abandoned his earthly body in Calcutta and became absorbed in Brahman.

Guru Dev's revival was carried on after his passing by his principal disciples, most notably Swami Hariharananda (popularly known as Swami Karpatri), Swami Shantananda Saraswati, chosen by Guru Dev to succeed him as the Śaṅkarācārya of Jyotir Maṭh, and Maharishi Mahesh Yogi, who spread Guru Dev's teaching around the world for over sixty years.

(For more detailed information on the life and teaching of Guru Dev visit the website of the Guru Dev Legacy Trust at **www.gurudevlegacytrust.com**).

4.0

Selected Discourses of Swami Brahmananda Saraswati

Swami Brahmananda's followers often took notes of his discourses. In 1947, the ashram published a collection of these discourses selected by Maharishi Mahesh Yogi in a book titled Śrī Śaṅkarācārya Vāksudhā. The Guru Dev Legacy Trust has translated all of the discourses in Vāksudhā to English and these translations are available on the Trust's website at **www.gurudevlegacytrust.com**. A print version is forthcoming.

Jugal Kishor Shrivastava assisted Maharishi in the preparation of Vāksudhā. Pictured below is a page of the draft text handwritten by Maharishi with minor edits by Jugal prior to the final printing at the Narmada printing press in Jabalpur in 1947.

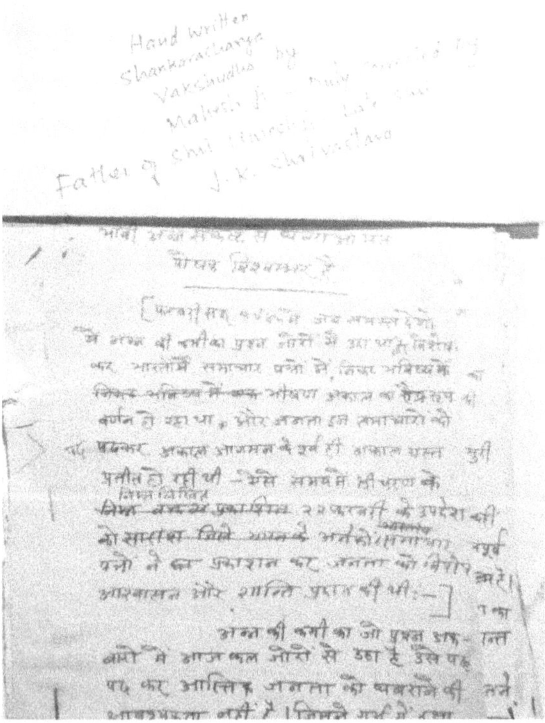

In reading Swami Brahmananda's discourses, it is useful for the reader to consider the time, place and setting to place them in their proper context. By the time Swami Brahmananda spoke the discourses, he had been installed as the Śaṅkarācārya of Jyotir Maṭh, the highest authority in Hindu life and religion (Sanātana Dharma). He closely adhered to traditional teaching, as augmented by his own direct experience of the highest spiritual truths.

Swami Brahmananda's audience lived in a culture deeply steeped in spirituality. The truths earlier revived by the great Adi Shankara and teachers of other great traditions were still widely known and respected. Although many aspects of this knowledge had become distorted and misunderstood, most Indian seekers were grounded in the general concepts and were always eager to gain a fuller, more true understanding. As Maharishi Mahesh Yogi once wrote: "Indian soil has witnessed many times the revival of life's true philosophy. The people of India have never hesitated to return once more to the right path whenever it was convincingly pointed out to them that their way of life had taken a wrong course. The receptiveness to Truth of the Indian people has always been a source of inspiration and a signal of hope to all movements aiming at the revival of true life and living."

While Maharishi adjusted Swami Brahmananda's teachings to a modern, Western-oriented world steeped in science, Swami Brahmananda's discourses are presented in more directly religious terms, as was appropriate given his audience. Although his teachings are wrapped in the traditional Hindu culture and scriptures, they contain universal truths that remain highly relevant today.

What follows are samples of the words spoken by Swami Brahmananda in his evening discourses.

VARIOUS QUOTES BY GURU DEV

"Until the desire to attain Īshvara (God) becomes unwavering, one will be flying and wandering around like a kite, not knowing where, lost in circles of innumerable passions."

"The threads of myriad desires must be gathered and unified to make a thick rope of devotion to Bhagvān and, with the help of that, one gains release from the circle of saṃsāra."

"The omnipresent, omnipotent controller of the world is Paramātmā. Establish your strong relationship with Him."

"Only through spiritual practices does Bhagvān manifest."

"You need not search for Bhagvān anywhere far away. Have faith and pray to Him with a naked heart. He is always with you and even within you."

"After your ego has been merged in Paramātmā then the individual existence is mingled with the universal existence and the whole universe becomes one's own."

HOW TO DESTROY VĀSANĀS (LATENT IMPRESSIONS, HABITUAL TENDENCIES, STRONG DESIRES)

This is written in relation to destruction of vāsanās–"Since decades the practice of worldly desire is prevalent; even though it is illusive, it cannot be destroyed until we practice for a long time." (Muktika Upaniṣad)

And related to this practice it is written –

"It is not possible to conquer mind with desire without practicing." We get to know the method of practice from a sadguru (real teacher). To achieve this always be on a lookout for sadgurus and learn from them the art of practicing in order to master the mind. Then practice regularly. By doing this, moss accumulated from multiple births will be wiped away and one can realise the true nature of sat-cit-ānanda (ultimate transcendent reality). Then life becomes contented.

There are of two types of vāsanās—auspicious and inauspicious.

It is written –

"The river of desire flows in two directions—auspicious and inauspicious, sometimes in auspicious and sometimes in inauspicious direction."If the heart is filled with tāmasik thoughts (quality of darkness, dullness), the river of desire flows in inauspicious direction. On the other hand, if filled with sāttvik thoughts (quality of purity) it flows in auspicious direction.

It is necessary to build a barrier in the name of Bhagvān (God) against the inauspicious direction. Building a barrier in the name of Bhagvān can be explained like this. When in the core of heart tāmasik thoughts increase, and when influenced by lust, anger, greed, delusion, passion, jealousy (the six inner enemies), improper thoughts arise. At that time we should start doing kīrtan (singing name and glory of God) or japa (reciting God's name) or bhajan (song in praise of God) or reading the Rāmāyaṇa or Gita.

By chanting the name of Bhagvān or singing the glories of Bhagvān we can overcome inauspicious thoughts. By using the name of Bhagvān as a barrier, the flow of the river of desire towards inauspicious path can be stopped. Then there will be only one auspicious way left for it to flow. After that, only auspicious thinking will rise in the core of our heart. This will make our deeds auspicious also. Gradually, the rise of inauspicious vāsanās in the core of heart, which give birth to inauspicious deeds, will cease forever. In this way inauspicious vāsanās will cease to exist.

Now for the complete destruction of vāsanās (latent tendencies) it is necessary to restrain the auspicious vāsanās too. The beautiful way to do this is to dedicate the auspicious vāsanās, and the good acts that come from them, to Bhagvān. The river of good desire, after merging with the ocean of God's shelter, will take the form of the ocean. Then it will lose its name and form and will not have its separate identity. This means if we undertake the practice of devoting auspicious vāsanās and the auspicious deeds coming out of them to Bhagvān, then the mind will be primarily occupied by vāsanās for Bhagvān.

Gradually auspicious vāsanās welling up in the core of the heart will be diminished too.

And by continuously practicing, the river of auspicious vāsanās will transform into an undivided stream of vāsanās only related to Bhagvān.

At that time, in the heart, freed from both auspicious and inauspicious vāsanās, the complete realisation of sat-cit-ānanda will arise. And the human being then achieves his real nature and the essence of ātmā. The human being will become contented and even self-realized.

In order to destroy vāsanās, the false vāsanās are to be controlled by remembering the name of Bhagvān and by summoning the help of good vāsanās. Finally, good vāsanās should be dedicated to God. For worldly people, this is the easiest way of giving up of desire. This is also the meaning of Niṣkām (without desire) Karma Yoga.

OWNERSHIP OF THE THREE WORLDS

We find several evidential examples in the Itihāsas (the two epics the Rāmāyaṇa and the Mahābhārata) and the Purāṇas (legendary mythologies of ancient India). The message from these is that one must establish an intimate connection with the Supreme Self (Paramātmā), which is the abode of all, the all-powerful controller of the world, and realise that He alone pervades all that is moving and unmoving (animate and inanimate, sentient and insentient).

By means of upāsanā (worship, pūjā, meditation, bhaja, nāma japa) prescribed in the scriptures, one becomes unified with the Supreme Consciousness. With this, mastery over the material elements—fire, water, air etc.—is naturally established. By gaining authority over the three-fold course of movement in time, viz. past, future, present, one gains ownership over the whole of creation.

WHETHER BHAGVĀN IS NIRĀKĀR OR SĀKĀR?

Once at Itawa a visitor asked – Is Bhagvān nirākār (without form) or sākār (with form)? Śrīcaraṇ explained him in this way:

"Bhagvān is both nirākār and sākār. Just as butter without form is present in each and every molecule of milk, Bhagvān, being nirākār, is present in the whole universe in every movable and immovable thing. By churning milk, butter takes its form. Similarly, by churning with the help of the churning stick of spiritual practice, one can realise nirākār Bhagvān as sākār Bhagvān.

GIVING UP OF POSSESSION

While giving a discourse at Prayāg, Śrīcaraṇ (Guru Dev) said:

There was a paṇḍit in Kāśī who was a great admirer of Rāmāyaṇa. He was very versed in Rāmāyaṇa, and often went for satsaṅg. Once he had the opportunity for a private meeting. He said, "Mahārāja! We spend the whole day turning the mālā beads and recite so many stories of Bhagvān, but our mind doesn't become calm."

Śrīcaraṇ replied: "It is evident that you have not dedicated your mind completely to Bhagvān. If the mind is dedicated to Bhagvān, then Bhagvān takes care of the mind. Then you don't have to be concerned whether it is calm or not. Since you are having concerns, it is obvious that you are still maintaining possession over your mind. And while you maintain possession of the mind, what then have you dedicated to Bhagvān? When you surrender possession of the mind, then Bhagvān can possess it and take care of it. Only one can have possession of something at the same time. Either you keep possession of your mind and govern it on your own, or you completely surrender possession and give it to Bhagvān. Then you become free of concerns as to whether the mind is settled or unsettled. Bhagvān will do whatever he thinks is right." One sādhu wanted a little piece of land from a landlord to build a hut of his own on the bank of the river Sarayū, but the landlord was not ready to give it to him. Once Śrīcaraṇ was passing by there. So, the sādhu came and said: "The landlord pays special homage to you, he will give the land if you talk to him." Śrīcaraṇ asked the landlord the reason for not giving the land. He said, "Bhagvān! I don't have any objection to giving the land. I could give the land even today; but the entire city's garbage gets dumped over there. In order to remove garbage from there we will have to face troubles from everyone." Śrīcaraṇ replied, "Why do you bother about removing the garbage. The one to whom you give the land will manage it himself. Just give up your possession of it, that's all, and then your responsibility is over. Hearing this, the landlord immediately gave the land.

Śrīcaraṇ said, "The significance of this is that when one's possession over mind is removed, then the garbage which is the agitation of mind is removed by the one who takes it. If the mind being dedicated to Bhagvān in this way still remains restless, this means the mind has not been dedicated completely. We should dedicate our mind completely to Bhagvān—should remove our possession over it completely—then our responsibility is over. And then there is no need to get agitated for a settled or unsettled mind."

"The other name of attachment is possession. The relationship between mind and saṃsāra (world, cycle of birth and death) through the bond of vāsanās (latent tendencies, strong desires) is only attachment. The root cause of this is the ego. Therefore as long as you have not dedicated your ego to Bhagvān, so long your possession over mind cannot be completely removed. And without Bhagvān having full possession over mind, the restlessness of the mind cannot be removed, and without removing of the mind's restlessness the state of peace cannot be realised. Therefore giving up of possession is the root cause of highest peace.

"Just as the worldly meaning of giving up possession is making a donation, so the supreme meaning of giving up of possession is real bhakti (devotion).

"After your ego has been merged in Paramātmā, the individual existence is mingled with the universal existence and the whole universe becomes one's own.

"When a river has entered the ocean and become completely merged with it, it acquires the qualities of the ocean. In the same way, when the source of vāsanās of the individual ego has been dedicated to the vast, bottomless ocean in the form of Paramātmā, then in that moment it gets the power of Paramātmā. But the dedication of the mind to the full nature of Paramātmā does not happen instantly. The miserliness of human life of previous births has long been ongoing. In order to get rid of this, the authors of the shāstras have told that there are eight more introductory steps before complete Self-devotion. These are the nine steps of navadhā bhakti (mentioned in various scriptures like Rāmāyaṇa) out of which complete devotion of the Self is the last. Complete Self-devotion is the very climax of bhakti. When one has dedicated all one's possessions to Bhagvān, then one has established an indiscriminate relationship with Him and at the end one becomes the very nature of Bhagvān. But only he gets this ability when he goes attentively through all the eight steps of bhakti step by step according to the rules in order to enter the final ninth stage. Success is not attained by attempting to lessen the characteristic features of bhakti by unauthorized arbitrary means of pūja (worshipping), pāth (reading), bhajan (devotional singing), kīrtan (chanting), etc. Therefore, having understood the process of devotion according one's own competence from a Sadguru and sticking to it, then only can the desired success be obtained by entering into the pure form of bhakti.

ALWAYS IN THE LAP OF BHAGVĀN

(The gist of this discourse was given at the time of the Śivarātri festival in Bhāgīrath Palace after the historical śatmukh koṭi homātmak mahāyajña" in 1943 in Delhi.)

If we think Bhagvān is far away from us, then He will go further and further away. But if we carry out our spiritual practices thinking He is within us, then He will always stay very near to us. When a woman carries water, one hand holds the pot of water on her head while the other hand remains free to hold her child, and when the child tries to climb on her, she lifts her child to her hip with her free hand. In the same way, Bhagvān, while taking care of the whole world, always keeps one hand free to lift or help His devotees. Just fall at His feet crying and He will lift you up and place you on His lap. You need not search for Bhagvān anywhere. Just have faith in Him and pray to Him from the depth of your heart. He is always with you, within you. You just need to understand how to carry out your spiritual practices and do your duties. Then you can feel that you are always on the lap of the Almighty with infinite power, bliss and joy.

www.ingramcontent.com/pod-product-compliance
Lightning Source LLC
Chambersburg PA
CBHW051520120626
46551CB00012B/1015
* 9 7 9 8 9 9 1 5 5 8 8 0 8 *